CAMBRIDGE MUSIC HANDBOOKS

Mahler: Symphony No. 3

CAMBRIDGE MUSIC HANDBOOKS

GENERAL EDITOR: Julian Rushton

Cambridge Music Handbooks provide accessible introductions to major musical works, written by the most informed commentators in the field.

With the concert-goer, performer and student in mind, the books present essential information on the historical and musical context, the composition, and the performance and reception history of each work, or group of works, as well as critical discussion of the music.

Other published titles

Bach: Mass in B Minor JOHN BUTT
Beethoven: *Missa solemnis* WILLIAM DRABKIN
Berg: Violin Concerto ANTHONY POPLE
Handel: *Messiah* DONALD BURROWS
Haydn: *The Creation* NICHOLAS TEMPERLEY

Mahler: Symphony No. 3

Peter Franklin
Lecturer in Music,
University of Leeds

The right of the
University of Cambridge
to print and sell
all manner of books
was granted by
Henry VIII in 1534.
The University has printed
and published continuously
since 1584.

Cambridge University Press
Cambridge
New York   Port Chester
Melbourne   Sydney

Published by the Press Syndicate of the University of Cambridge
The Pitt Building, Trumpington Street, Cambridge CB2 1RP
40 West 20th Street, New York, NY 10011-4211, USA
10 Stamford Road, Oakleigh, Melbourne 3166, Australia

First published 1991

Printed in Great Britain at the University Press, Cambridge

British Library cataloguing in publication data

Franklin, Peter.
Mahler: Symphony no. 3. (Cambridge music handbooks).
1. Austrian symphonies. Mahler, Gustav, 1860-1911
I. Title II. Series
784.184092

Library of Congress cataloguing in publication data

Franklin, Peter.
Mahler: Symphony no. 3 / Peter Franklin
p. cm. – (Cambridge music handbooks)
Includes bibliographical references and index.
ISBN 0 521 37071 X. – ISBN 0 521 37947 4 (pbk)
1. Mahler, Gustav, 1860-1911. Symphonies, no. 3, D minor.
2. Symphonies – Analysis, appreciation. I. Title. II Series.
ML410.M23F7 1991
784.2' 184–dc20 90-25620 CIP

ISBN 0 521 37071 X hardback
ISBN 0 521 37947 4 paperback

For Nicholas Cann,
teacher, friend – in fond memory
8.7.91

That something new was in the course of preparation in the arts, something that was more passionate, more problematical, more alluring than all that had satisfied our parents and the world around us, was the particular experience of our young years. Fascinated by this one aspect of life, we did not notice that these transitions in the aesthetic realm were nothing but trends and foreshadowings of more far-reaching changes, which were to shake the world of our fathers, the world of security, and finally to destroy it.

Stefan Zweig (1881-1942), writing of his boyhood in late nineteenth-century Vienna in *The World of Yesterday*, p. 55

My symphony will be something *the world has not had before!* The whole of nature finds a voice in it and reveals profound mysteries such as one might perhaps intuit in dreams!

Mahler on his Third Symphony, to Anna von Mildenburg, July 1986. See H. Blaukopf (ed.), *Gustav Mahler Briefe*, p. 165 (footnote)

Contents

Contents

Plates

Preface

'What is the use of Mahler?', shouted the title of an article in *The Face* in November 1986.[1] Its author, Ian Macdonald, sketched some answers that boldly addressed the spiritual predicament of modern man just a few desultory page-flips from glossy fashion ads, articles on the current pop scene and sub-headings like 'In the new and brash City of London, money doesn't talk, it yells!' The effect of the piece in that context was not unlike what Theodor Adorno describes as the *Durchbruch*[2] (meaning a rending or 'breaking through') that Mahler's own music strives towards, its impetus courting interruption, as if by a voice from outside. The article vouched for the powerful communicative impact of such dislocation, even when as destructive as that found in the finale of the Sixth Symphony:

> Audiences, especially, of late, *young* audiences, applaud this piece with the energy of startled recognition. In its violent extremes of feeling, its relentless desire to be undeceived, to see the human predicament as it really is, it sums up so much of our experience of the world.

The unselfconscious use of the present tense and the collective 'our' point to a range of issues, aesthetic and otherwise, that Mahler's symphonies raise. They seem bound up with our world in a rare way, from mass-marketing (recently of motor oil) to movies, through matters of taste and intellectual history into the innermost privacy of emotional life. His Third, completed in 1896, is a six-movement colossus including settings for solo voice (of Nietzsche, in the fourth movement) and chorus (of a folk-poem from *Des Knaben Wunderhorn* in the fifth). It is not currently the best known or most frequently performed of the cycle; only in 1961 did it receive its British premiere, in St Pancras Town Hall.[3] Yet its attempt to scale the mountain of musical tradition in search of the unique and all-embracing masterpiece secured Mahler one of his first really significant, if strongly contested, successes with a new work. It is also, alongside the Eighth, a symphony in which he felt that he had come close to answering the metaphysical questions that plagued him; a work of grand public ceremonial, instinct with Wagner's vision of the music-drama as a focus for quasi-religious social renewal. The contradictions and tensions of his musical style, once facilely diagnosed as 'neurotic', were resolved in a musical tribute to the ancient notion of the Great Chain of Being as reinterpreted by nineteenth-century German philosophy in the wake of the Romantic movement.

My purpose here is to try to unfold, in context, the story of how Mahler came to conceive that a symphony might give voice to 'the whole of nature' and what that might have meant within late-nineteenth-century musical culture. For this reason, the detailed history of the work's composition is not presented until after its background and contemporary reception have been discussed. My aim has been to avoid doing what Mahler himself detested: merely 'analysing' it as a model symphony, ripe for inclusion in examination syllabuses. Instead, it is viewed as part of a dynamic process that tended not only towards the completed work as a final goal, but also towards the utopian resolution grandly enacted in differing, perhaps even contradictory ways in its outer movements and other, later-composed symphonies. Mahler would have understood Ian Macdonald's exhortation in *The Face*: 'If you're not prepared to risk having your life changed, you shouldn't mess about with art.' Many of his statements indicate that his major works, even at their own expense, both depicted and sought to change the life from which they had sprung. Uncovering the dynamic and complex interweaving of expression and aspiration in the Third Symphony will occupy me more than any attempt to prepare it for the pantheon.

I acknowledge a debt to the University of Leeds, whose research grant, combined with a sabbatical term in 1989, facilitated the writing of this book and the chance to study sketches for and the manuscript of the Third Symphony in the Pierpont Morgan Library in New York. The staff of that library, particularly Mr J. Rigbie Turner, are thanked for their quiet efficiency. The grant also helped fund a trip to The Hague to look at Willem Mengelberg's scores of the Third and Fourth Symphonies in the Dutch Musical Archive. The assistance of its curator, Dr Fritz Zwart, is most gratefully acknowledged. Professor Gottfried Scholz of the *Hochschule für Musik und darstellende Kunst* in Vienna solved a problem of Viennese dialect. Dr Edward Reilly of Vassar College, Emmy Hauswirth of the *Internationale Gustav Mahler Gesellschaft* in

Vienna and Patricia Duage of the *Association Gustav Mahler* in Paris all responded generously to my various enquiries. Others who have helped include David Cooper, Susan Haase-Derrett, Charlotte Purkis and Paul Bulger, the last of whom long ago permitted me time to think and the Gold Room in which to do it.

All references will be to the *Kritische Gesamtausgabe* score of the Third Symphony, edited by Erwin Ratz for the International Gustav Mahler Society of Vienna (*Sämtliche Werke,* Vol. III, Universal Edition, Vienna 1974 (UE 13822)), which has the added merit of bar-numbers. Where possible, reference to the cue numbers printed in all editions of the score will also be made. Some of the music examples have been adapted from the four-handed piano reduction of the symphony by J. Wöss (Moscow 1973). For illustration material I am indebted to the Pierpont Morgan Library (for the opening page of the manuscript of the final movement), to Stanford University Libraries, Department of Special Collections (for the early sketch page for the first movement) and to Samuel Schweizer of Zäziwil, Switzerland, who supplied the excellent photograph of the inn and lakeside summer-house on the Attersee, in Upper Austria, where the Third Symphony was composed.

Part I

The symphony in its world

I

Background: progress, tradition and ideas

For one last time, in Raimund's plays, everything returns to life that had appealed to my youthful imagination: the Baroque world I had seen in palaces, churches and waking dreams, the world of gods, genii and daemons. Here spirits stand equal to bourgeois philistines; while nobles in their mansions appear no more solid than the gods. Theatrical perspectives ample enough to portray the universe, to hold up a mirror to the whole panorama of existence, are necessities when one is young and poor.

Oskar Kokoschka [1886-1980]: *My Life*[1]

The Austrian painter Oskar Kokoschka was writing here of a 1940 design commission for the revival of three early nineteenth-century Viennese plays. He recalls his formative experience of a world of art that was not only encountered in theatres, art galleries, schools and churches. It also extended into an inner landscape of shared images and fantastic possibilities, where the poor might rub shoulders with the rich and great. One might even turn fantasy into reality by becoming an esteemed practitioner of art oneself and holding up one's own truthful-fantastic mirror to the 'panorama of existence'. Yet by the time of Mahler's death in 1911 Sigmund Freud, also in Vienna, was darkly relating artistic motivation to 'the same conflicts which drive other people into neurosis and have encouraged society to construct its institutions'[2] and Kokoschka had become an alienated modernist with a confused sense of why, and for whom, he might actually produce paintings:[3]

Society in general – the world my friends and I referred to as 'The Adults' – possessed varying conceptions of art. The middle class, in whose eyes I was still a standing offence, viewed art as something to decorate a wall. For the nobility it was an adjunct of their ancestor cult, to be used like the Court Photographer. The workers had more pressing priorities than that of employing creative artists: higher wages, shorter working hours, the task of strengthening their own organization, and one day, if possible, becoming a State within a State.[3]

Many books have been written about culture in turn-of-the-century Vienna[4]. It was the geographically central capital city of an Empire whose ruling dynasty, the Habsburgs, had first gained power in the Austrian kingdom of the late 13th century. The reigning Emperor, Franz Joseph I, had come to the throne in 1848 and, since his coronation as King of Hungary in 1867, was 'Imperial and Royal' monarch of the whole of Austria-Hungary, his processions a regular sight in Vienna. An immeasurable historical past ceremonially surrounded its modernists of the *fin de siècle*, meeting in fabled coffee-houses where Hofmannsthal, Klimt, Schoenberg, Karl Kraus, Freud, Wittgenstein, even Adolf Hitler, might have been encountered almost simultaneously. These quoted recollections of Kokoschka succinctly evoke the artistic obsession of those times in a way that is directly relevant to any attempt to understand the Austrian-rooted Mahler. He was born in 1860 in Austrian Bohemia: by present criteria a German-speaking Czech Jew (Moravia, where the family moved soon after Mahler's birth, was also in the Austrian part of the Empire). Like many provincials who were later drawn in to the capital, Mahler embodied something of the complex reality of the multi-national state.

He was thirty-six when he finished the Third Symphony in 1896 and living in the north-German port and city-state of Hamburg. In 1891 he had become first conductor at the *Stadttheater* there, after a series of increasingly important posts in German and Austro-Hungarian theatres. Mahler was nevertheless returning to Austria for the summer vacations during which most of his composing was done and he was periodically planning ways of returning to Vienna and the great Court Opera Theatre, in spite of its institutional anti-semitism. The Third stands at a crucial turning-point in his career. Even while completing it his Viennese aspirations and machinations were coming to fruition and within a year he would indeed be Director of the Court Opera (1897). Reflecting both a critical attitude towards Tradition and Mahler's strong desire to become a master-of-ceremonies of the traditionally constituted culture in which he worked, the Third is a document of potent cultural-historical interest.

Music and nineteenth-century culture

Late-nineteenth-century Art was capable of functioning either as a celebration of the way things were or as an arena for the rehearsal of what might be. One might also seek to draw the two together, to infuse the blood of the New into the partly loved, partly hated body of the established Old. Wagner's

Gesamtkunstwerk had presented the blue-print for just such a synthesis. His mature music-dramas, from *The Nibelung's Ring* (first performed complete in 1876) to *Parsifal* (1882), and his detailed theoretical and philosophical writings, were taken as gospels of a new artistic creed by all manner of young artists and intellectuals in the last three decades of the nineteenth century. The very fact that they seemed so clearly to divide audiences into conservative detractors and modernist enthusiasts only convinced the latter all the more of the vitality of their radical content. To side with Wagner was to relive the revolutionary aestheticism of Schumann's earlier *Davidsbund*, united in an esoteric comprehension of Beethoven's greatness against the sterile, uncomprehending Philistines[5], for all that their money might support the concert season.

The social and artistic climate that developed during Mahler's student years in Vienna offers itself readily to the broadened repertoire of approaches available to late twentieth-century musicology, no longer condemned to talk about music history as a linear progression of Great Works. Learning from cultural critics like Theodor Adorno, interdisciplinarians like Marc Weiner and from historians like William Weber[6], we have grown more used to discussing musical culture as a network of institutions and practices, even though this means that the professionally fetishized musical 'work' has at times to be moved from the centre of the picture before we can reconstruct a contextually relevant understanding of its meaning. Music involves both more and less, historically speaking, than melodies, modulations and chains of influence amongst its producers. It also provides highly charged opportunities for social interaction, for class distinctions to be both blurred and defined by 'taste', for careers to be furthered and for people to express indirectly things which dominant norms might not otherwise permit. Equally, the very forms of this Music must potentially include not only symphonies, cantatas and operas, but also the simple song whose initial notes alone might awaken a covert or open community of patriotic or political feeling. Then, too, there are the bells, children's choirs, marching bands and café trios that make up the full paraphernalia of social musical activity: the sounds of a large and complex society at worship, going to war, or simply celebrating a public holiday.[7]

When musicology was concerned with cultural prescription, on the basis of an accepted canon of specific artistic treasures or models of excellence, such things were, of course, considered less than wholly serious and banished from the consideration of what music was about. Such a view of music is itself now a valid object of historical study and can be seen to have been struggling for dominance in the very period with which we are concerned. It carried with it an absolutist or 'idealist' view of the art as something transcendent, of its nature 'above' expressive involvement with matters political, intellectual or even emotional. In his widely influential, oft-reprinted 1854 treatise on musical aesthetics entitled *Vom Musikalisch-Schönen*, Eduard Hanslick, the subsequently famous Viennese music critic, had even asserted that music, philosophically speaking, was only 'about' music. He went on consistently to suggest that while questions of determining historical context might be relevant to the art-historian, they were irrelevant to the 'aesthetic inquirer' into music, who was concerned with models of transcendent formal excellence and must therefore distance himself not only from the titillating effects of Wagner, but also from any music whose charms, like those of some of Verdi's or Donizetti's themes, were 'fit only for low music-halls'.[8]

Music was thus in fact selectively pure, its aestheticians, no less than its composers, divisively enmeshed in an aristocratically orientated class society. Around 1900, Mahler's complex and changing attitude towards the partisan issue of symphonic 'programme-music' (meaning music openly descriptive of ideas or events) reflected his conscious involvement in the politics of a musical culture divided between youthfully immoderate Wagnerian programmaticists and the establishment-endorsed idealism of conservative classicists. There is no clearer indication of the extent to which Mahler felt that his Third Symphony both reflected and participated in the issues of contemporary cultural politics than the excited reports on its conception and near-completion that he gave Natalie Bauer-Lechner in early July 1896. Anticipation of establishment hostility and incomprehension recurs like an *idée fixe*. He would, he said, not live to see the first movement 'recognised and appreciated for what it is', but would have to suffer like Christ on the Mount of Olives on its behalf; not a hair of his head would be left unscathed: 'all the critics will pelt me with stones again, and one of them (as after the First to Marschalk) will say: "This Mahler is either a genius or a crackpot!" But I am certain: a crackpot!'.[9]

Six years later Mahler wrote a careful explanatory letter to a prospective conductor of the Third Symphony, in which he cautiously made sure that his correspondent had a correct list of the original movement-titles and understood the essential metaphysical nature of the work's programme: leading 'from the gloomy rigidity of merely elemental being (the forces of Nature) – to the delicate creations of the human heart which in turn point the way and extend out above and beyond all this (to God).' Only then did Mahler ask him to avoid referring to the titles in his pre-concert talk: 'it is not unimportant for the future of this, as of my other works, that it should be made "public" in the right way. May you succeed in becoming a model for others with your seriousness of purpose.'[10]

What is clear from this letter is how far Mahler, two years after his much-reported 1900 declaration of hostility to all descriptive musical 'programmes'[11], adhered to his original conceptual understanding of the symphony's content, while being concerned not to jeopardize the work's continuing success by injudicious publicity. Such concern about his creative progeny might have been determined on more than one level by his own experience. As the talented son of petit-bourgeois provincial parents, and one who had made good in a rare and remarkable way, Mahler would have been critically aware of the potential relationship between music, social success and 'doing things right' in the cultural environment in which he worked. In 1895, although first conductor at the opera in Hamburg, Mahler had yet to rise to the highest executant position in the Royal and Imperial Court Opera of Vienna. He seems still to have toyed, however humorously, with the unlikely notion that he might succeed economically and socially as a creative musician, even telling Natalie Bauer-Lechner, as he started his summer-vacation work on the Third: 'With it, I hope to earn applause and money ...'[12]

By the next day, however, Natalie records that Mahler had reverted to a more alienated realization that his particular kind of musical idealism manifested itself in a way that would probably be incomprehensible to symphony-concert promoters and audiences: 'You know as far as money-making goes, the Third won't do any better than the others! For, at first, people won't understand or appreciate its gaiety; it soars *above* that world of struggle and sorrow in the First and Second, and could have been produced only as a result of them.'[13] Here we encounter the late-Romantic composer as the proto-modernist whose inner path of spiritual and artistic development leads him away from, or somehow 'beyond' the day-to-day world and the conventional expectations of his audience. We also encounter in Mahler, to return to the deeper determinants of his concern about the public presentation of his works, the problematic matter of his being an assimilated Jew: the kind of Jew who, in a time of rising anti-semitism in Vienna, would habitually distance himself from any special allegiance to the Jewish community, having even become a convert to Christianity (he was baptized into the Roman Catholic Church in 1897). Such Jews came to dominate the cultural life of late nineteenth-century Vienna and thus bring into the foreground of its self-image a socially located sense of tension and inner contradiction.

In a short study of Mahler specifically from the angle of his Jewishness,

Henry Lea has applied to him the term 'marginal man', derived from the sociologist Robert E. Park and depending upon a characterization of the Central European Jew as a person who

> ... veered back and forth between submission and defiance, between vying for acceptance and fighting the establishment, with inevitable consequences for his personality, self-esteem, mental health and of course his relationship with Gentiles. Because he continually looked at himself through the eyes of others and was uncommonly concerned with injustice, he often developed a hypersensitivity and emotional intensity that Gentiles found difficult to accept.[14]

Such generalizations have a certain value, but fail in Mahler's case to account for the extent to which his private creative intensity and sense of isolation were to be experienced within artistic culture as central, rather than marginal, to the generation of Kokoschka. They also fail to explain the way in which entrenched opposition to his works and ideas, as to those of Freud and other prominent Viennese Jews of the period, underlined that centrality to a complicatedly divided and increasingly unstable society. To approach a deeper understanding of his paradoxical, non-marginal marginality, we must turn for assistance to an important contextual study of Mahler and the Third Symphony.

McGrath's approach

The historian William J. McGrath's *Dionysian Art and Populist Politics in Austria*, published in 1974,[15] not only drew together detailed discussion of artistic works and philosophical ideas in a cultural and political context, but also presented the intellectual history of a cohesive *group* of people, or rather an interlocking series of groups. At their centre were the subsequently influential politicians Engelbert Pernerstorfer and Victor Adler, founder members during their school days in the 1860s of an idealistic, German-folk-culture orientated society in which embryonic forms of some of their later ideas were discussed (Adler was to become leader of the leftist Social Democratic party). While not initially subscribing to a clear political programme, the circle's members rapidly developed a strong antipathy towards the liberal bourgeois values of their parents' generation and embarked, with many of their contemporaries, on a path of discovery that would embrace both socialism and a strong sense of anti-Austrian, anti-Habsburg, Germanic nationalism.

The bourgeois liberalism Adler and Pernerstorfer came to oppose was essentially what we would now call 'conservatism'. For all its concern with the freedom of the middle- and upper-class individual, it depended upon a *laissez-faire* belief in market forces and non-interventionist government, linked with a network of paternalistic moral and cultural values that seemed increasingly bankrupt in the face of changing political, social and economic realities. The Viennese Jewish writer Stefan Zweig (1881-1942) has vividly described the anti-youth, repressively adult-dominated culture of his own schooldays and its shock at the appointment of so young a man as Mahler (aged 37) to the directorship of the *Hofoper* in 1897[16].

The new, youth-orientated culture represented by men like Mahler or, more dramatically, the teen-aged Hugo von Hofmannsthal (1874-1929) publishing poems under the pseudonym 'Loris', fostered a secret-society atmosphere that had formerly impinged upon the public arena only in large-scale student organizations like the *Leseverein der deutschen Studenten Wiens* (Reading Society of Viennese German Students). Founded in 1871, it gradually drew members of the Pernerstorfer circle into its organizational administration as its anti-bourgeois, anti-liberal concerns – for the unity of a nationalistic German *Volk*, for passionate feeling as opposed to materialistic or 'scientific' reason, for social concern and political intervention – turned increasingly to Schopenhauer, to Wagner and the young Friedrich Nietzsche for philosophical guidance. From Schopenhauer[17] came the pessimistic vision of the phenomenal world as the manifestation of an underlying 'Will', whose violence and selfishness the human subject could overcome only by ascetic self-denial. From Wagner, particularly through Vienna's youthful Academic Wagner Society (founded in 1871), came the philosophical framework for a new concept of the role of art, and of the artist as 'poet-priest' of a new, German-folk-myth rooted and socially binding religious art. Its musical and 'dionysian' roots in ancient Greek tragedy were then to be explained by Nietzsche in his Wagner-dedicated *The Birth of Tragedy*, first published in 1872. Of particular significance to our interest in Mahler is the fact that it was in the first formal discussion of Nietzsche by the *Leseverein* (1875) that a contribution was made by the nineteen-year-old poet Siegfried Lipiner (1856-1911), a pupil of Fechner in Leipzig who would be hailed as a genius by Nietzsche himself after he had read Lipiner's *The Unbound Prometheus* in 1877.[18] Lipiner was to become an intimate friend and mentor of the young Gustav Mahler, who in that same year of 1875 began his studies at the Vienna Conservatory, aged fifteen.

Mahler must have come into contact with Lipiner around the time of the latter's 1877 report to the *Leseverein* on Nietzsche's 'Schopenhauer as Educator' and his important 1878 lecture 'On the Elements of a Renewal of Religious Ideas in the Present', in which he praised the decline of dogma and the renewal of myth, leading to a new, trans-individual pantheism: 'then are we Pan, the all-one and then are we Theos, the divine ... Yes, we must transform, transform and be transformed'[19] In fact the *Leseverein* was officially disbanded by government order in that very year (1878), but its influence and wide membership within the University of Vienna (a number of whose professors belonged) would have been encountered directly by Mahler when he first took some university courses in 1877-8 (including Greek art and a study of the Mediaeval German of Eschenbach's *Parsifal*).[20] That influence would still have been tangible when he returned to the University in 1880, registering for such Nietzsche-related courses as classical art, archaeology, the history of philosophy and the philosophy of Schopenhauer.[21]

By this time Mahler had come into direct contact with members of the Pernerstorfer circle through his lifelong friends Albert and Nina Spiegler and had been 'taken up' by the relatively wealthy socialist Victor Adler (a Jew who had converted to Protestantism). Mahler seems to have become well integrated into the idealistically Wagnerian, pan-German circle of young socialist literati and artists surrounding the Pernerstorfer luminaries. Richard von Kralik was to recall a meeting of the circle (including Pernerstorfer himself, Victor Adler and the historian Heinrich Friedjung) at which, with Mahler at the piano, the company had 'joined in singing *Deutschland, Deutschland über alles!* to the piano accompaniment of *O du Deutschland ich muß marschieren*'.[22] In 1881 he had even participated in the founding of one of the circle's internal literary-philosophical societies – the 'Saga Society', led by Kralik and Lipiner, whose goal, according to Kralik, was to be 'living, thinking and working in myths, gods, and heroes as, say, the ancient Greeks and the ancient Germans'.[23] It is apparently at a meeting of the Saga Society in Kralik's house that we encounter Mahler early in Natalie Bauer-Lechner's *Recollections*, playing the overture to *Die Meistersinger* for an assembly of Wagnerian socialists and (in Natalie's case) at least one future crusader for women's rights.[24]

Radical conservatism

The balance between radical and conservative impulses in the Third Symphony demands careful reading, however. Mahler's public opposition to 'programmes' after 1900 matched his persistent devotion to the respected form of the Symphony, and in the opera-house his paradoxical aim, like Wagner's, was always that of an idealistic, anti-populist opponent of 'mere theatre'. In the late 1890s he was still a marginalized composer (conveniently stamped as a Straussian modernist) but an increasingly prominent conductor: the socialist sympathizer who could nevertheless terrorize the worker-players of the orchestras he conducted like some Dickensian schoolmaster in the name of a relentless idealism. He was also the idealistically aspiring symphonist whose works might nevertheless be dismissed as 'cheap novels' by more conservatively inclined composers.[25] Mahler, the outcast-achiever, was a central representative of his changing culture, with all its contradictions and sense of old certainties painfully lost. The Hamburg critic Ferdinand Pfohl, who had known him as both exasperatingly otherworldly and ambitiously self-absorbed during the period of the Third Symphony's composition,[26] recalled him fancifully as a half-daemonic creature out of one of E.T.A. Hoffmann's Romantic tales:

> He looked like one who had questioned God and had accordingly been cast out of the Light and into the Darkness, one whose crime was knowledge and who now sought with desperate urgency the way back to the lost paradise ... seeking to reach God and the angels on the sounding bridge of music which joins the present world with the hereafter.[27]

The revolutionary, *critical* aspect of Mahler's music, which then, as now, could upset Brahmsian conservatives, consisted not least in the way in which it articulated Faustian questioning as much as it embodied the harmonious reconciliation that even Romantic classicism had tended to consider the primary function and purpose of the art. Whereas E.T.A. Hoffmann's fictional Kapellmeister Kreisler had regarded music as an 'angel of light' which 'lifts me victoriously out of myself',[28] the Mahler who could appear to his contemporaries as a kind of real-life Kreisler also drew into his music the Kreisleresque personality: 'a seething volcano, capable at any moment of erupting with destructive fire, consuming all mercilessly.'[29] It was the precise way in which he did this, beyond any problematic 'programmaticism', that gave his music its conceptual force and clarity and thus almost inevitably made it unacceptable on principle to a conservative music-aesthetic orthodoxy with a vested interest in the direct equation of music with the exemplary models of 'organic unity' produced by Viennese classicism (liberally extended back to Bach, but forward only to the early Romantics and Brahms).

These models were rudely confronted in his Third Symphony. It was not that Mahler hadn't done his strict counterpoint; not that he didn't revere the

German Masters; not that the movements of the Third couldn't be reduced to a conventional tonal scheme (the F major conclusion of the first movement, in a symphony in D, poses only a small doctrinal problem). It was just that in all other respects it bore 'modernism' and 'experimentalism' blazoned all over itself in unseemly, popular-sounding march-tunes, licentious sonorous effects and an epically elaborated 'misunderstanding' of sonata form as a programmatic conflict between opposing kinds of musical material. For these crimes Mahler not unreasonably expected that 'not a hair of my head will be left unscathed'.

Inspiration and Nature (Schopenhauer, Wagner, Nietzsche)

... imagine such a *great work,* in which in fact the *whole world* is mirrored – one is, so to speak, no more than an instrument on which the Universe plays, I tell you, in some places it strikes even me as uncanny; it seems as if I hadn't written it at all.[30]

Statements like this, about the Third Symphony, are a telling indication of the complex way in which part of the whole dynamic of Mahler's creative work in the 1890s was nevertheless rooted in the ideology of orthodox classical aesthetics, where the greatest art was considered an unmediated manifestation of Nature. Yet he conceptualized that ideology in the extravagantly heightened manner of one who did not quite belong. His Promethean outbursts of aspiring art-enthusiasm clearly indicate that he sought, like the young Kokoschka, to 'hold up a mirror to the whole panorama of existence'. Such enthusiasm was always ready to embrace art not simply as a calming image of reconciling stability, but as the medium of *disruptive* revelation.

The fiery idealism of Mahler's concert music was complicatedly at odds with both social and musical convention. This was certainly the case in his First Symphony of *c*.1884–8. Its powerful thrust towards a triumphant union of self and nature, apparently bypassing society altogether, was conceptually prepared in the famous letter of 1879 to his youthful friend Joseph Steiner. It was written from a dispiriting summer-job as family music-instructor on a Hungarian country estate.[31] Opening with a harangue about 'the hideous coercion of our modern hypocrisy and deceit' and 'the unbreakable links that exist between life and art', Mahler had come to the point of declaring a suicidal intention before being swept away by an involuntary love of Nature, with its 'blue skies and swaying flowers'. But then the mood of the youthful *fahrender Gesell'*, encountered in the song–cycle and the first two movements of the First Symphony, had given way to a grand Faustian apostrophe in which the mood of the symphony's Finale, and much to follow, was explosively expressed:

> O that a god might tear the veil from my eyes; that my clear gaze might penetrate to the deepest reaches of the earth! O that I could see this earth in its nakedness, lying there without adornment or embellishment, just as it lay before its Creator; I would then step forth and face its genius. 'Now I know you, deceiver. With all your feigning you have not deceived me; not blinded me with your illusions! Behold! A man strong and unbowed, in spite of your playful, gibbering deceits and the terrible blows of your scorn! May fear strike you, wherever you hide! From the valley of mankind the cry goes up to your cold and lonely heights! Do you comprehend the unspeakable misery here below that for aeons has been piling into mountains? And on their peaks you sit enthroned and laugh! How will you answer for all this one day before the Avenger, you who have not been able to atone for the suffering of a single tormented soul!!!

To understand how Mahler came to equate the quest of the youthful Avenger with that of the aspiring Composer, we might turn back to those writers in admiration for whom he found such close community with Lipiner and members of the Pernerstorfer circle. Central amongst them were Wagner and Schopenhauer, of course. Alma Mahler was later to attest to her husband's belief that 'on the *essence* of music, apart from Wagner, in *Beethoven*, only Schopenhauer in *Die Welt als W[ille]. u[nd]. V[orstellung]*. had anything valuable to say'.[32] Mahler's interest in *Beethoven* (in 1892 he gave a copy of it to his Hamburg friend Dr Arnold Berliner)[33] is important, not least for the reason that it represented Wagner's most extended attempt to interpret Beethoven's significance in the direct light of Schopenhauer's philosophy, in the centenary year of the composer's birth (1870). In it, Wagner elaborated on the philosopher's view of music as a metaphorical picture of the dynamic inner nature of the world (as Will), as a revelation of the 'essential nature of all things'.[34] What Wagner did not take over from Schopenhauer was the philosopher's rather fixed, Mozart- and Rossini-orientated understanding of what music was. Instead, a major part of the essay was devoted to the theoretical description of the art as historically *evolving* towards the point where it might indeed be regarded as a revelation of something 'natural', which for Wagner meant a transcendent music 'emancipated from the influence of fashion and fluctuating taste, and elevated to an ever-valid, purely human type'.[35] Music attained only with Beethoven the role that Schopenhauer had conceptually prepared for it:

> We may deem it certain that our civilisation, as far as it determines artistic man, can only be reanimated by the spirit of music – of that music which Beethoven released from the fetters of Fashion. And the task of leading the way in this sense to the new and more soulful civilisation, which perhaps may shape itself under that spirit, as well as the new religion permeating that civilisation – that task must be reserved for the German spirit.[36]

I have indicated already how positively, and for what reasons, radical young Austrians might have sympathized with Wagner's requirement that the new, socially transforming 'religious' music had to be *German* in spirit. In 1893, the year after he had given a copy of *Beethoven* to Arnold Berliner, Mahler felt unreservedly able to hail Wagner, in conversation with Natalie Bauer-Lechner, as a daunting but ever-inspiring 'firebrand ... a revolutionary and reformer of art such as had never existed before!'[37] The whole tone and drift of Wagner's programme was clearly of the utmost formative significance to Mahler, who would later respond to enquiries about his religious belief with the statement: 'I am a musician; everything else is covered by that.'[38] But Mahler was to become a far from slavish Wagnerian in his own creative work *outside* the opera-house. Here we need to consider more closely the kind of 'modernism' with which he was widely associated by his contemporaries – an issue which must inevitably lead us to the question of his attitude towards the modernists' favourite philosopher: Nietzsche (1844-1900).

No discussion of this issue can avoid confronting the celebrated passage in Alma Mahler's memoir where she recorded Mahler's shock, in 1901, at discovering an edition of Nietzsche on her shelves, and his command that she throw it into the fire.[39] This attitude can, I suspect, be fully understood only in the light both of his initially awkward, schoolmasterly relationship to the girl he would shortly marry and of the increasing outward conservatism to which he seems to have inclined, for a multiplicity of reasons, during the last decade of his life. Those reasons cannot occupy us here, however, where the object of our interest is a symphony written at the height of the anti-Christian and also anti-Wagnerian influence of Nietzsche on youthful modernists; a symphony which set words from his most popular work, in which are recorded the intellectual odyssey and teachings of a poetic philosopher to whom Nietzsche gave the ancient name of 'Zarathustra'.

Here is Mahler in a letter of 1896 (to Max Marschalk). He is discussing the symphony as a post- as much as pre-Wagnerian form:

> We now stand – I am certain of this – at the great parting of the ways, where the divergent paths of symphonic and dramatic music will soon become obvious to anyone with a clear notion of the nature of music. – Even now, if you compare a Beethoven symphony with Wagner's tone-pictures, you will have no trouble in recognizing the essential difference between them. – Indeed, Wagner took over the *expressive means* of symphonic music, just as now the symphonist who is fully aware of and at home in his medium will lay claim in his turn to the expressive riches gained for music through Wagner's efforts.[40]

This might lead us to assume that his divergence from Wagner was a simple function of his Wagnerian belief in the evolutionary 'progress' of music. It was a belief that Mahler had charmingly and revealingly expressed in a letter to Gisela Tolnay-Witt in 1893. Although only eight or nine years old, she had had the presence of mind to ask why modern composers needed such an extravagantly large instrument as the nineteenth-century symphony orchestra with which to express themselves:

> As time passed ... the composer began to include more and more profound and complicated parts of his emotional life in his work – until the *new era* in music started with Beethoven.
>
> ... music became more and more common property – audiences and performers increased steadily. Instead of the chamber there was now the concert hall; instead of the church, with its *new instrument,* the organ, there was the opera house ... we moderns need such a large apparatus to express our thoughts, be they large or small. First, because we are often forced to distribute our numerous prismatic colours upon various palettes, to protect ourselves against misinterpretation; secondly, because our eyes learn to see more and more colours and ever finer and more delicate modulations in the rainbow; thirdly, because in order to be heard by the multitudes in huge concert-halls and opera-houses, we have to make a big noise.[41]

Wagner is not specifically drawn into Mahler's picture here, whose evolutionary scenario nevertheless extends the concept of the religious-communal aspect of the new art by stressing the increasing democratic availability of music. Its ever more subtle expression had become 'more and more common property' in institutions that, like the opera-houses, in some way superseded churches. There is certainly little in the way of conventional idealism in this formulation, which deals in music as the bearer of 'extra-musical' conceptual and emotional content as if Hanslick had never been.

It was his desire to constrain free emotional expression within a critical conceptual framework that could have drawn the anti-sensualist Mahler to Nietzsche's later writing on Wagner. For Nietzsche, Wagner had failed in his quest for Beethovenian universality precisely because of the skill with which he had expressed, and the uncritical way he had abandoned himself to, his own psychological peculiarities of feeling and fancy. The power of the Germanic and bourgeois world of *Tristan* and *Parsifal* to draw others into its pained and passive hedonism led Nietzsche, the former Wagnerian acolyte who had dedicated *The Birth of Tragedy* to the Master, to reach the following conclusions in *The Case of Wagner* (1888):

> Wagner represents a great corruption of music. He has guessed that it is a means to excite weary nerves — and with that he has made music sick. His inventiveness is not inconsiderable in the art of goading back into life those who are half dead. He is a master of hypnotic tricks, he manages to throw down the strongest bulls ...
>
> We know the masses, we know the theatre. The best among those who sit there — German youths, horned Siegfrieds, and other Wagnerians — require the sublime, the profound, the overwhelming ...
>
> They are quite right, these German youths, considering what they are like: how *could* they miss what we others, *we halcyons* miss in Wagner — *la gaya scienza;* light feet, wit, fire, grace; the great logic; the dance of the stars; the exuberant spirituality; the southern shivers of light; the *smooth* sea — perfection.[42]

Mahler made, to my knowledge, no direct reference to Nietzsche's anti-Wagnerism. It is, however, inconceivable that he was not aware of it or had not in some way come to terms with it in his 'epoch-making' (as he initially described it)[43] reading of the philosopher between 1891 and 1896, the year in which he completed the Third Symphony. Many of Mahler's comments about it indicate familiarity with Nietzsche's earlier description in *The Birth of Tragedy* (1872) of the 'Apollonian' and 'Dionysian' forces in Greek drama. These complementary principles were clearly modelled on Wagner's initial theory (modified in *Beethoven* in favour of music) of the music-drama as a union between stage action and the subterranean utterance of the orchestra. For Nietzsche, Apollo's taming and ordered poetic expression filtered violent Dionysus's vision of Nature's underlying chaos. The Apollonian artist was therefore the medium between things 'as they are' (meaning for Nietzsche at that time more or less the Schopenhauerian vision of a world governed by a blind and impulsive Will) and a dream-picture conducive to a state of mind in which one might go on living. The projections of the Apollonian art-illusion were compared by Nietzsche to the dark spots we see after gazing too long at the sun, but here the effect was reversed, so that they became 'necessary effects of a glance into the inside and terrors of nature; as it were, luminous spots to cure eyes damaged by gruesome night'.[44]

From this early formulation of the quasi-religious socio-psychological role of Greek tragic art, and by extension of the artist in general, Nietzsche was to move towards a conception of human consciousness and metaphysical truth that held artistic man to be the creator, or 'dreamer' of the world. The following is from the book whose title, *Die fröhliche Wissenschaft*, Mahler was for a time to adopt for the Third Symphony:

> How wonderful and new and yet how gruesome and ironic I find my position vis à vis the whole of existence in the light of my insight! I have discovered for myself that the human and animal past, indeed the whole primal age and past of all sentient being continues in me to invent, to love, to hate, and to infer. I suddenly woke up in the midst of this dream, but only to the consciousness that I am dreaming and that I must go on dreaming lest I perish – as a somnambulist must go on dreaming lest he fall...
>
> I, too, who 'know', am dancing my dance ... the knower is a means for prolonging the earthly dance and thus belongs to the masters of ceremony of existence ...[45]

In *Also sprach Zarathustra* (1883-5, although its four parts were first published together only in 1892), Nietzsche was, as he felt, to redeem man, emancipated from the idea of God, from pessimistic fatalism of the kind that periodically haunted Mahler (who in darker Schopenhauerian moments could ask 'Have I really willed this life, as Schopenhauer thinks, before I even was conceived?').[46] This redemption came in Zarathustra's doctrine of 'eternal recurrence': which suggested that before and after every moment of time there must be an eternity in which all that is possible, including that very moment of experience, must already have occurred and be going to repeat itself an infinite number of times. To will and love the fact that he must 'return eternally to this identical and self-same life, in the greatest things and in the smallest'[47] would be, for the man of the present, to acquire a new kind of moral responsibility for his own, and indeed all, life.

This world-view – vehemently espoused by Mahler as a form of reincarnationism[48] – was clearly rooted in *The Birth of Tragedy's* Dionysian vision of nature as a purposeless chaos which the artist alone, seen now as prototypical *Übermensch*, could usefully 'redeem' in Apollonian illusion. For Nietzsche, art represented the only means of making *sense* of life and of ourselves as

images within it.[49] Its expressive content, however, extended beyond individual subjectivity, as it did in the Dionysian chorus of Greek tragedy, into a
collective creative picture of nature-as-dream. Nietzsche's argument consistently led him to value not Wagnerian opera, but the 'naive' folk-song as the
most fundamental 'musical mirror of the world' available to his own culture.
He even cites Arnim and Brentano's collection of 'Old German Songs', *Des
Knaben Wunderhorn* (*The Youth's Magic Horn*, 1808-6), as a specific source of
ever-renewable artistic insight:[50]

> Anyone who ... examines a collection of folk songs, such as *Des Knaben
> Wunderhorn*, will find innumerable instances of the way the continuously gen-
> erating melody scatters image sparks all around, which in their variegation,
> their abrupt change, their mad precipitation, manifest a power quite unknown
> to the epic in its steady flow.

The programme and popularization

The early Mahlerian symphony utilized a form whose development
through Liszt and Berlioz in the direction of the Wagnerian music-drama had
tended always towards the semantic depurification and popularization of
musical processes; towards gestural highlighting and intensification of the
conflictual, 'Beethovenian' formal type. The model was that of the long-
esteemed social symphony: the 'playing together' whose goal remained the
reconciling Grand Finale (even if diabolically frustrated, as in Berlioz's
Symphonie Fantastique). Yet from Beethoven's Ninth onwards it had been
progressively colonized, particularly in the first movement, by Romantic lit-
erature in the form of the Faustian internal monologue of individual self-
questioning or 'struggling against Fate'. This was presented as a dramatized
attempt either to heal or to highlight the rift between increasingly sharply
differentiated blocks of musical material.

In Mahler, *what* was to be reconciled, and the conceptual nature of that
reconciliation, grew ever more extreme. The programme itself was undergo-
ing a significant development in which social implications were not lacking.
He explicitly conceived of the Second Symphony as progressing from individual anguish over the meaning of life (in the first movement) to an egalitarian moral-metaphysical resolution on the apocalyptic Judgement plains,
onto which had marched 'The great and the little ones of the earth – kings
and beggars, righteous and godless'.[51] The Mahler who could claim that 'It
is only when I experience that I "compose", only when I compose that I
experience!'[52] could hardly have conceived of musical problems as being sep-

arate from those of life itself. His own verbal explanations of his works, whose creative process seems necessarily to have been one of constant conceptual and musical cross-fertilization, nevertheless grew both more complex and more terse. As no more than 'signposts and milestones',[53] the cryptic titles and descriptions were intended to aid the imaginatively reliant listener in the creation of his own explanatory programme. This was not invalidated by the divergence of its narrative content from Mahler's or anyone else's (Mahler himself suggested a variety of contrasting explanations for his early symphonies). What mattered was its metaphorical relevance to the musical experience, whose fundamental symbolic significance might be grasped in numerous verbalized descriptions. Mahler believed that music should be apprehensible by anyone, whatever his or her conceptual and expressive capacity as bestowed by class, taste or education. His public attitude towards 'programme-music' may have varied, but the subversive implications of this view found tangible artistic realization in the Third Symphony to an extent that is clearly indicated by its critical reception, particularly when all descriptive titles and explanations were suppressed.

Reception: the early performances

Whatever his own later feelings about the philosopher, there is ample evidence that Mahler continued to be regarded by others as a 'Nietzschean' modernist after 1896, whether positively or negatively depending on the critic's own attitude towards musical modernism and its implications. Nowhere are these points more strikingly illustrated than in William Ritter's response in 1901 to the Fourth Symphony (the one we now tend to regard as Mahler's most classically balanced and even 'conventional'):

> It's no consolation to me to think that the feeling of revulsion that rose in my soul upon hearing this work was shared by a good half of the calm and serious Germany that applauds absolutely safe, not to say totally reliable musicians ... That which blinded my friends and me was everything about it that seemed to us to be merely self-advertisement; the way in which it constantly appealed to the lowest instincts of the crowd and so expertly caressed, aroused and incited the sensuality latent in each one of us to indulge itself; it was the breeze of contagious madness that made one shriek with laughter; the constant overloading and the perversion of an alluring melody with every possible large and small sound effect; the way it swung from the sublime to the ridiculous, in an apparent effort to please everyone from the aristocrat down to the peasant; the way in which its Jewish and Nietzschean spirit defied our Christian spirit with its sacrilegious buffoonery and the fact that it exasperated our loyalty to the past by crushing all our artistic principles to a pulp.[1]

What Ritter heard, in the year *before* the premiere of the Third Symphony in 1902, was no charming divertissement in the classical manner. Instead, he found himself assailed by a music that seemed to transgress all the laws of decency, propriety and taste – and the hierarchical social order which they helped support. It was certainly no simple matter of 'modernism' versus 'conservatism' in any comfortable intra-musical fashion. Ritter's response to the Fourth Symphony, like the consistently fractured and contradictory reactions to the Third from 1902 onwards, tends powerfully to validate later contextual readings of Mahler as the self-conscious spokesman of a fragmenting culture – readings which find their most profound and challenging articulation in Theodor Adorno's 1960 study of Mahler, for all that it is still viewed with varying degrees of suspicion and ignorance by British and American Mahler-scholarship.[2] It was Adorno who first persuasively described Mahler's dual internalization of and challenge to the tendency of the consolidating bourgeois tradition to banish the plebeian voice to the realm of ' folklore'; his tendency to produce music which acts as a 'showplace for collective energies' beyond the moment of private sentiment; his subversion of the language of musical 'universality' by speaking, as it were, in dialect ('Mahler's tone has a "flavour" in the way that the Riesling grape is considered "flavoursome" in Austria').[3]

Such issues were not merely implicated in the culturally conditioned conceptual underpinning of the Third Symphony; they were sharply focussed in Mahler's lifetime in both public and critical response to it as a musical experience, with or without any indication of the original programmatic conception. Before looking more closely at the history and nature of that response, however, it is worth considering the broader critical placing of Mahler that was emerging around 1900, when he began to be written about seriously as a composer; to appear in the pages of contemporary studies of 'modern music' and even to merit monographs in his own right. The first such monograph, written by Ludwig Schiedermair in 1900, even opened by setting Mahler specifically in the context of the Bohemian, and by implication Jewish, people, in whose art 'Germanness is mixed with Hungarian elements, in which the sounds of the far East are also heard.'[4] Mahler is then described as a philosophically-inclined composer, who, although individual, belonged to the modernist camp of Germans like Max Schillings and Richard Strauss. Interestingly, Schiedermair presents him as a *Tondichter,* rather than a composer of fully 'absolute music', who was nevertheless ideologically opposed to elaborate published programmes. He hails Mahler as an idealist ('in our realistic times')[5] who was set against the decadence of post-Wagnerian music. Given the latter point, it is particularly interesting that Schiedermair should conclude his study with two aphorisms drawn from the opening pages of Nietzsche's *Also sprach Zarathustra.*[6]

The reason why he should have done so may be further explained with the aid of another book that had appeared earlier in 1900 and was referred to by Schiedermair in his monograph for its lengthy quotation of a letter of Mahler's discussing the issue of programmaticism. It even seems to have been the unauthorized publication of this letter to the music-critic Arthur Seidl, in Seidl's *Moderner Geist in der deutschen Tonkunst,*[7] that had been the root cause of Mahler's lively protestations in the celebration after the Second Symphony performance in Munich (October 1900). He had energetically encouraged the gathering of friends and critics (which included Seidl and Schiedermair, who reports it in his monograph[8]) to 'have done with programmes'.[9] The letter in question was the famous one of 1897 in which Mahler described the circumstances of the inspiration for the conclusion of the Second Symphony's finale. In it, he had agreed with a point that Seidl had put to him: 'You are quite right that my music arrives at the programme as *final ideal clarification,* whereas with Strauss the programme *pre-exists as a given task.'*[10] Annoyed to find this published, Mahler was to claim that his answer had been more in the nature of polite homage to Seidl and Strauss than a truly considered formulation.[11] Still more interesting about Seidl's book, however, was the broader context in which he set his discussion of Mahler as an exponent of 'The Modern Spirit in German Music'.

Seidl was particularly interested in the problem of how to place Mahler *vis à vis* Strauss, to whom his book was dedicated. In it, Seidl took Strauss as his key modernist precisely on the grounds of the latter's avowed creative and intellectual sympathy with Nietzsche on the progressive, revisionist path of post-Wagnerian music (what Seidl called 'left-wing' Wagnerism as opposed to the more dutifully conservative, 'right-wing' Wagnerism of Humperdinck and others).[12] For Seidl, a minor Nietzsche-scholar in his own right, Nietzsche represented the prototypical 'modern character': 'a focus in which all the beams of the light of modern life appear to have been gathered up'.[13] Nietzsche was the Wagnerian turned anti-Wagnerian, the tearer-down and rebuilder; above all he was the passionate polymath, at once philosopher and psychologist, artist and priest, thinker and poet. While admitting that he had not yet enough to go on to make any clear or final assessment of the astonishing appearance of Mahler in the musical firmament, Seidl, the committed Straussian, offers as his best shot the suggestion that the two stem respectively from complementary 'northern' and 'southern' streams of Germanic musical culture:[14] Strauss from a northern tradition stretching from Bach through Beethoven to Wagner, Mahler from a southern one embracing Handel, Cherubini and Liszt and tending, we might assume, in the direction prescribed by Nietzsche in his demand: *'Il faut méditerraniser la musique.'*[15]

Early performances of movements from the Third Symphony

The first music from the Third Symphony to reach the public ear was that of the second movement. It was sufficiently uncontentious to score a success in Berlin – a city that was rarely friendly towards Mahler's music and would give the rest of the symphony a dusty reception later. When it was given there by Nikisch on 9 November 1896, the Minuet was warmly applauded and critically welcomed to an extent that Mahler had never before experienced with a first performance. It was introduced by Mahler himself in an interesting little programme-book which advertised the Berlin premiere of Strauss's *Also sprach Zarathustra* (also completed in 1896) for the next Philharmonic concert of 30 November.[16] The note, signed 'G.M.', is interesting in many ways as representing Mahler's first public announcement of the general scheme and nature of the work he had completed that summer. Beneath the concert item number (IV), ascribed to 'Gustav Mahler, Kapellmeister am Stadttheater in Hamburg', the movement was presented as

Was mir die Blumen auf der Wiese erzählen
aus der Symphonie, in F Dur (III) ' Ein Sommermorgen-Traum'

[What the flowers in the meadow tell me
from the Symphony in F major (III) 'A summer-morning dream']

There then followed five musical examples, described successively (and extremely economically) as 'Main theme with ever more richly unfolding variations:', 'From which develops:', 'A 2nd theme:', 'A 3rd theme:' and 'Coda:'. The note then concludes as follows, presenting the symphony's 'programme' in its characteristic and consistent form (of which there are many versions) as a series of movement-titles:

Die Symphonie besteht aus folgenden 6 Sätzen:

Einleitung: „Pan erwacht"

No. 1.	„Der Sommer marschirt ein". (Bachuszug.)
No. 2.	„Was mir die Blumen auf der Wiese erzählen". (Menuett.)
No. 3.	„Was mir die Thiere im Walde erzählen". (Rondeau.)
No. 4.	„Was mir der Mensch erzählt". (Altsolo.)
No. 5.	„Was mir die Engel erzählen". (Frauenchor mit Altsolo.)
No. 6 (Schlusssatz).	„Was mir die Liebe erzählt". (Adagio.)

[The symphony consists of the following 6 movements:
Introduction: 'Pan awakes'.

No. 1.	'Summer marches in'. (Bacchic procession.)
No 2.	'What the flowers in the meadow tell me'. (Menuett.)
No 3.	'What the animals in the forest tell me'. (Rondeau.)

No 4.   'What man tells me'. (Alto solo.)
No 5.   'What the angels tell me'. (Womens' chorus with alto solo.)
No 6 (Finale). 'What love tells me'. (Adagio.)]

There is no mention of Nietzsche here, and by comparison with the bold title of Strauss's forthcoming 'symphonic poem' this movement-list looks no more programmatic or subversively modern than a piano album of descriptive genre-pieces for young ladies. Certainly further performances of the second movement *Blumenstück* in 1897 (20 and 21 January in Leipzig under Nikisch; 31 March in Budapest under Mahler) continued to be warmly received, with few adverse critical comments. Not so the repeat performance of the movement in Berlin on 9 March 1897, when it was accompanied by the third movement and final Adagio of the symphony. The former, with its subsequently infamous posthorn solo (described by Paul Moos as sentimental: a 'weak, uninteresting melody') immediately alerted the Berlin critics to the fact that there was more than mere charm and contrapuntal ingenuity in this symphony (Moos had appropriately characterized the second movement as 'so good-mannered ... so thoroughly saccharine, that at least the easily corrupted ladies take pleasure in it').[17] In addition, the performance under Weingartner followed closely in the wake of a Berlin lecture by the conductor which was later to be incorporated into his *Symphony Writers since Beethoven (Die Symphonie nach Beethoven*, first published 1897). The short section on Mahler included the following assessment by Weingartner (three years Mahler's junior):

> One may, without definable cause, find bizarre, even ugly elements in his works. One may be put off for a time by a sense of prolixity and surfeit, perhaps by the often insufficient self-criticism in the selection of thematic material ... But everything he [writes] bears the stamp of strong feeling, rich imagination and a glowing, almost fanatical enthusiasm even where, instead of controlling it, he allows himself to be completely carried away by it.[18]

Whatever the decisive reason, the Berlin critics echoed in a series of negative and scornful reviews the boos that had been clearly audible amidst the applause that greeted the three movements. And with that, apart from the Budapest performance (for the first time in public by Mahler himself) of the *Blumenstück* at the end of March, the career of the Third Symphony was effectively terminated for five years, the first, fourth and fifth movements still unperformed. It was a period in which Mahler made little public headway as a composer, until the significant triumph of the Second Symphony under his baton in Munich on 20 October 1900. Suitably impressed, and before the embattled first performances of the Fourth in 1901, Richard Strauss decided to arrange for the full premiere of the Third Symphony. It would take place on 9 June 1902, on the penultimate day of the annual Festival of the *Allgemeine Deutsche Musikverein* (of which Strauss had just become President) in the small Rhineland town of Crefeld (now Krefeld); Alma Mahler records the event in some detail.[19]

The first performances of the complete symphony

Since its founding by Liszt in 1859, the *Allgemeine Deutsche Musikverein* had been associated more or less exclusively with the 'New German' school of programmatic composers, and its Festival remained an ostensibly anti-Brahmsian modern affair,[20] which in 1902 included works by Schillings, Reger, Pfitzner, Humperdinck and Strauss. Mahler's First Symphony had been performed, also at Strauss's instigation, at the 1894 Festival in Weimar. The audience in 1902 would naturally have been prepared for innovation. It is nevertheless clear that the Third achieved a conclusive public triumph whose echoes, if somewhat confused, even reached the July edition of *The Musical Times* in London: 'Much interest was created by the performance, under the composer's direction, of the new symphony in D minor by Gustav Mahler, the director of the Vienna Opera, the final movement of which, introducing a choir of boys' voices, with contralto solo, produced a most marked impression.'[21]

The modernist sympathies of the audience and its excited reception of the work highlight the special interest of Mahler's concern to idealize and even 'conventionalize' the Third in public (on this occasion he need hardly have done so), while always seeking to clarify its conceptual or 'programmatic' nature in private communications with friends and critics. Response to the work must be judged in the light of the fact that all programmatic elucidation – specifically the titles and the narrative key to the third movement that had apparently been available in Berlin in March 1897[22] – was suppressed in advance of the concert. On the other hand, we need to be aware not only of the barrage of images and explanations with which Mahler bombarded his friends while composing the work, but of the letter he wrote (in 1901?) to Schiedermair, who was to be commissioned to write a programme-note for the Crefeld premiere. Mahler commented warmly on the latter's monograph of 1901, but wished to set him straight about the fact that the Third 'has nothing to do with the struggles of an individual ... it is Nature's path of development (from stiff materiality to the greatest articulation! but above all the *life of nature!*)'.[23] In the end, one can only be struck by the continuing tension between Mahler's new public presentation policy and his private conceptual interpretation of the symphony[24]; further still by the fact that none of his public strategies fooled the critics for one moment into thinking that they were hearing anything other than an altogether radical new work, the suppression of whose programme some even denounced as adding the insult of evasion to the injury of an apparently chaotic eclecticism of style and taste.

Indeed, from the start of the complete symphony's significantly successful public career up to 1904, audience pleasure was matched at best by confusion, at worst by downright hostility and personal denunciation from a majority of the critics. The local Rhineland reporters provided the most balanced reviews of the first performance. Those writing for national periodicals like the always conservative *Allgemeine Musik-Zeitung* or *Die Musik* seemed much more inclined to be negative, although even here grudging recognition of the enthusiastic audience reception is encountered (the Adagio, in particular, was almost universally praised, however faintly). The many reviews cited by Henry-Louis de La Grange in the second volume of his Herculean biography of the composer[25] establish a subsequently consistent repertoire of positive and negative observations. On the positive side, we read of the exciting new work of an original genius, a prodigious, absolute master of the orchestra, who writes in a 'clear and intelligible' language, with 'modesty ... and naivety'. The 'utterly serious' work is described as concluding with a particularly fine and noble Adagio and achieving in all a 'glorious victory' for the composer.[26] On the negative side, we read of the stupefying and disconcerting first movement, banality, a lack of melodic invention and originality, linked to eclecticism and an absence of any sense of 'inner necessity' about the music. It included 'bizarre and trivial elements', atrocious cacophony, 'incomprehensible platitudes' and rudely garish sounds which added up to chaos, even the order of the movements seeming arbitrary.[27]

Given that there had apparently been something of an anti-Mahler campaign at the Festival prior to the performance, the audience's enthusiasm clearly played its part in modifying the reaction of some critics who might otherwise have been more inclined to condemn the symphony. As a result, there are signs of a judicious mixing of comments from both the positive and the negative ranges. There is as yet no clear demarcation between reviews pro and contra on predictable party lines. Sixteen months later, two more performances of the Third in Amsterdam (22 and 23 October 1903), again under

Mahler, at the invitation of Willem Mengelberg, seemed further to confound his worst fears about the work. Once more, it was a resounding success with the audiences, even winning over orchestral players terrified in advance by stories of Mahler's tyrannical manner as a conductor.[28] Here one of the most interesting responses was that of the passionate Wagnerian Alphons Diepenbrock, a composer and classical scholar who, in best modernist fashion, was also a committed Nietzschean. He had, however, been disappointed by Strauss's *Also sprach Zarathustra*. The materialistic, *Gründerzeit* chauvinism of the New German school he found opposed to the 'Great German' spirit (*Gründerzeit* was the term applied to the period of rapid expansion and financial speculation, 1874-1914). Diepenbrock had been equally shocked to hear in advance of Mahler's own desecration of Nietzsche by linking words by him with texts from *Des Knaben Wunderhorn* (in the fifth and, by association, third movements). After hearing the symphony and getting to know its composer, however, he was fully converted, even to the point of being able to overcome an initial distaste for the 'many ugly features' in the first movement: 'He is modern in every way. He *believes* in the future ... his music appears to be granted the ability to "transform people" and to give the experience of "Katharsis".'[29] Whereas the materialist Strauss seemed to him to be in touch with heaven only by inter-city telephone, Mahler's more authentic spiritual universality resisted the former's 'neo-Prussian coating'. He could be considered a quite other and more naive kind of artist in the Third, 'thanks to the many folksongs [Volkslieder] (and a splendid women's chorus taken from *Des Knaben Wunderhorn*)'.[30]

Diepenbrock's congratulatory definition of Mahler's modernism as comprising both idealism *and* a tendency towards an eclectic musical popularism proved a rare insight. It was to find few echoes in the reviews that attended the Third's generally less well received performance in Frankfurt just over a month later (2 December, 1903). There the work was found 'complicated' and 'incomprehensible'. The *Frankfurter Zeitung* critic in particular was astonished to find in the middle of a serious composition a kind of 'parade of the guard', along with grotesque and vulgar effects.[31] Such effects, however, proved no obstacle to the sensational progress of the Third Symphony through nine cities in 1904. Mahler even found himself invited to conduct it in Prague by Angelo Neumann, whose programming, as de La Grange points out,[32] was rarely prompted by idealistic motives. It was in Prague (25 February, 1904) that Diepenbrock's evaluation of the work was to be echoed in a subtle assessment by Richard Batka:

Mahler has the courage to be vulgar. He needs this element against which to set off the rest, which is important. He deserves to be warmly applauded for this. In this way concert music leaves the paths of allegory to find new powers and vital impulses. Perhaps the introduction of a cornet solo playing *Die Post im Walde* in the scherzo is a facile effect, but nonetheless magical... Didn't Bach, Haydn and Beethoven draw abundantly from the realities and banalities of everyday life, even in their symphonies?[33]

This is clearly addressing an established and already polarized debate, in which the weight of critical opinion is set against the blatant intrusion of the musical *vox populi* in Mahler. Batka's answer is to turn its rude and disruptive effect into a strategic element in the 'classical' game of contrasts and oppositions, for all Mahler's tendency towards a kind of kitchen-sink musical realism (Batka nevertheless felt that the 'hymnic splendour' of the finale would, as it often did, 'convert the most determined enemies of new music').[34] At the end of November, 1904, Alex Winterberger, in the *Leipzig Neueste Nachrichten*, remained one of those thoroughly immune to conversion. He was reporting the performance of 28 November, in which Mahler conducted the Winderstein Orchestra (the conservative Gewandhaus Orchestra had no truck with new music). Denouncing the whole work as an 'oriental [implying Jewish] symphony' of 'tragico-fantastic ballet music', *he* considered the work's vulgarities as intentionally pandering to a disreputably popular audience. Mahler, he proclaimed, 'knows his public and knows perfectly what is needed to give them a moment's astonishment'[35] Offering a still bolder, and retrospectively fascinating, solution to the critical problem of the Third than either Batka *or* Winterberger, however, was the anonymous critic of the *Neue Zürcher Zeitung* who had attended the Zürich performance on 19 January 1904, under Volkmar Andrae. Criticizing the suppression of the programme, he went on to do precisely what Mahler on occasion advocated[36] and offered his own elucidatory programme to a symphony that he felt could in no way be heard as 'pure music'. It was, he suggested, a 'Volkssymphonie' in sympathy with 'the socialist movement' and expressing 'the life of the people of today'. A 'relentless struggle against the state and the forces of order' was followed, in the second movement, by a description of the intimate family life of ordinary people, whose social merry-making was the subject of the third movement. The voice of the solitary man (fourth movement) then gave way to the naive faith of the child, before finally discovering its well-being in divine love.[37]

The Third in Vienna

What is particularly important in all this is that the diverse interpretations were clearly based on a shared hearing of what the work *was*; of what the symphony 'expressed'. The evaluation that followed depended upon whether or not the critic believed symphonies *should* express such things, or whether, perhaps, one could somehow overlook them and appreciate it 'nevertheless' as an impressive musical construction. Relevant to earlier comments about Mahler's own ambivalent public stance is his particular liking for a review of the Third in Cologne on 27 March 1904, in which the anti-programmatic Otto Neitzel had suggested that the strangenesses of the work, including 'laughter of satanic scorn' and the 'cynical grating of teeth', were nevertheless not 'contrary to the universal laws of beauty'.[38] By the end of 1904 the battle-lines were well and truly drawn between the spokesmen of opposing views of a musical culture over whose established conventions and manners the Third Symphony seemed to ride rough-shod, while at the same time somehow confusingly aspiring to internalize and explain them. Nowhere were these divisions more pronounced or long prepared than in Vienna itself, where the Third was finally presented by the Philharmonic, during a rare period of calm in its stormy relations with Mahler, on 14 December 1904.[39]

Once again, what really inflamed the anti-Mahlerians was the clear and resounding public success the work achieved – so much so that the concert was repeated on 22 December. The Viennese critics had for the most part consistently condemned Mahler's compositions out of hand. Robert Hirschfeld, a fellow Moravian Jew who nevertheless opposed Mahler relentlessly in the *Wiener Abendpost*, accordingly directed his anger squarely at the audience who did not, he suggested, understand anything except novelty and the latest fashions. He denounced the work as striking 'poses in front of the mirror' and representing nothing so much as a 'back to Meyerbeer' movement. It was, in fact, 'Non-music without form or content'.[40] Even the progressive sympathies of Max Vancsa in the *Neue Musikalische Presse* were painfully stretched in a review that praised the 'classical' qualities of the movements comprising the symphony's second part, but he was baffled by the work's wider ambiguities:

> In the modern way, it is deeply divided and given to extremes. He has numerous artistic ideas, which he honours in succession, giving way to convulsive ecstasies as if before idols, only to mock and destroy them a moment later. The most fundamental trait of his being is irony, an irony which corrodes and destroys the listener who, thus far having willingly let himself be led by the

nose, suddenly finds himself completely sober, losing the thread altogether. The artist doesn't believe in himself and the listener doesn't believe in him![41]

There was, of course, a minority of positive critical voices, including those of Julius Korngold in the liberal *Neue Freie Presse,* Wallaschek in *Die Zeit,* and the socialist David J. Bach in the *Arbeiter-Zeitung,* the newspaper of Victor Adler's Social Democratic Party. We also have a moving description by Ernst Decsey of the performance and the way in which it won over the initially still sceptical students and younger modernists (including Schoenberg and his followers of the period).[42] But, as always, it is from the negative reviews that some of the most revealing historical insight is to be gained into how the Third was heard (without great surprise on his part) by Mahler's contemporaries. For this reason I return here to the articulate and, in many ways, brilliant Robert Hirschfeld, to whom Mahler's very name came to act like a red rag to a bull. His most remarkable critique of the Third was not written in 1904, however, but after the third Viennese performance of the work in 1909, in Mahler's absence (he had left the *Hofoper* in 1907 and was on this occasion already in New York for the winter season); the conductor was Bruno Walter.

It is worth pointing out that since the Graz performance of December 1906 – preceded by a lengthy explanatory article two days before, by Ernst Decsey, including the account of the 1904 Vienna performance referred to above – Mahler had permitted the original programme to be published once more.[43] Generally speaking, it was considered helpful in the understanding of so large and complex a symphony. For Hirschfeld, however, it simply provided ammunition for one of the great critical broadsides of the period, in which he agonizingly anticipated the insights of Adorno, but from a quite opposite moral and cultural perspective:[44]

Faithful friends of Gustav Mahler have made possible, by means of a subscription, the performance of his Third Symphony, which has already been given once in Vienna. Since the world we live in is not yet ready for works of this type, it proved difficult to fill the Musikvereinsaal ... [which] once again became the setting for one of those dionysian festivals which the Mahlerian bacchantes and maenads of Vienna go in for with frenzied enthusiasm. As the ancient Greeks needed their mysteries to liberate instincts restrained by a peaceful life-style ... so a Mahler symphony is now used by a post-Hellenistic society to release the explosive forces which have been pent up in quiet bourgeois [bürgerlich] duties and professions. Deranged by such explosions, the mind thoroughly upset by the tumult, it is impossible to engage in the least objective discussion. Bruno Walter – the most faithful of the faithful Mahlerians, most loyal of the loyal, most sincere of the sincere – recently proclaimed in hair-raising statements that the first movement of the Third 'doesn't have the character of the expression of a personality, but of a force of nature, a cosmic power [einer kosmischen Potenz]'. In art, others prefer human to cosmic powers. The exaltation of the old disciples of Wagner is now pushed to the point of caricature. The Bruckner fanatics can at least climb amongst sublime themes, which rise from an unfathomably deep temperament and are veritable marvels of inspiration. Now we turn to the pitiable thematic catalogue of the third Mahler symphony: an indigestible assemblage of ideas that are variously banal and studiedly awkward; interminable trombone exercises; the languid 'Post im Walde' (with, in conclusion, the sounding of the retreat); ironic funeral marches which, in all Mahler's symphonies, never cease to mock tears; peculiar ballet-motifs which Mahler was the first to introduce into symphonic music; eternal jubilation and sobbing [Juchzer und Schluchzer]; instrumental jokes which reduce all serious discourse to nothingness in a few measures. The joke-symphony – that's Mahler's special musical preserve.

Hirschfeld went on to extol those more dutifully conscientious musicians who still 'spend their entire lives trying to comprehend the secrets of late Beethoven ... the complexity of Brahms's craft'. The comparison could only be unfavourable to Mahler's works:

What significance do they have in the evolution of the symphonic art'? The question is evaded with familiar digressionary formulae like 'personality', 'expression of the times', of a 'cultural movement' ... One has only to examine two or three pages of a Mahler score: innumerable markings; directions; a cult of trifles and details, a nervous spasm in every tiny contrast; accelerandi, shifts of dynamics and sound-colour; incessant signals, miniature fanfares and motifs which, hardly heard, are tossed to other instruments before even acquiring their own colour. And it is this that captivates dilettantes and the unmusical in the symphonies of Mahler. In this agitation they think to find genius ... What does it mean to say that in Mahler's symphonies their epoch expresses itself? Isn't a new coat or a fashionable hat also an expression of the times? Every epoch has its strengths and weaknesses, its nobility and its insignificance, its honesty and its lies. The great symphonists feel and reveal the grandeur, the strengths, the nobility and the integrity – not the negative features – of their time. Yet how frivolous, childish and without strength our epoch appears in Mahler's symphonies, with their cowbells, their big and little bells, their rattles and their bunches of twigs, their jumbles of echoes and distant sounds, their bizarre sonorities – which don't even seem to have come from musical instruments. There is nothing in the sophistical explanations for these parodistic funeral marches, for these pensive yodellings and this ironic dance-hall music [Fünf-Kreuzer-Tanzes], this philosophical posthorn ...

We must combat the Mahler principle because it contains a danger. Because Gustav Mahler, whose gift is a specifically orchestral one, can only play with the emotions and fails to master the grand form. Thus the momentary effect, even if it is only a staccato semiquaver or a 'Luftpause', becomes an isolated goal in itself, the intonation more important than the note or the architectural structure.

Part II

The world in the symphony

3

Genesis and design

My calling it a 'symphony' is really inaccurate, for it doesn't keep to the tra-
ditional form in any way. But to me 'symphony' means constructing a world
with all the technical means at one's disposal. The eternally new and changing
content determines its own form. In this sense I must forever learn anew how
to forge new means of expression for myself – however completely I may have
mastered technical problems, as I think I may claim to have done.

Mahler on the Third Symphony, 1895.[1]

Just how new the content and form of the Third Symphony were is a question that must occupy us no less than it did contemporary critics. Some
authoritative hypotheses about the complex evolution of its formal ground-
plan have been developed by Susan Filler and subsequently reviewed by
Edward Reilly.[2] On the basis of the available sources, Filler has systematically
catalogued the stages of this evolution as reflected in Mahler's continued
shuffling of the order of the movements during the work's composition. To
make sense of this process, however, and of the bewildering array of Mahler's
commentaries, sketches, draft lists of movement-titles and annotations in the
manuscript, we must speculate about the unfolding imaginative conception of
the work that these sources might bear witness to. This cannot be considered
in isolation from that of the earlier symphonies. Whatever may be suggested
by the many subsequently discarded plans and versions of the work, it is a
fact of weighty significance that the Third should have ended up with a
structural plan that looks like a logical extension of the five-movement
scheme, disposed in two unequal parts, of the Second Symphony, shown in
Figure 1.

Both works are post-Beethovenian choral symphonies. In the Second, the
orchestral–choral finale has acquired a short, freestanding solo aria as a kind
of prelude. In the Third that is retained, but now the finale itself splits into
two: the choral part shrinks into a second prelude to the purely instrumental
Adagio. This was the one major new element in the scheme, whose presence
was to be significantly justified by Mahler on the grounds of its being a

Symphony II (1890-4)	Symphony III (1893?-6)
Part 1: 1 (Extended dramatic sonata structure)	Part I: 1 (Extended dramatic sonata structure)
– Pause –	– Pause –
Part II: 2 Andante	Part II: 2 Minuet
3 Scherzo (based on *Wunderhorn* setting)	3 Scherzo (based on *Wunderhorn* setting)
4 Alto solo (*Wunderhorn*)	4 Alto solo (Nietzsche)
5 Finale (orchestral apocalypse and resolving choral conclusion	5 Short choral movement (*Wunderhorn*)
	6 Finale (symphonic Adagio)

Figure 1

'higher' musical form, for reasons we will come to. Any inclination we may have to see the underlying five-movement structure (even the First Symphony had originally been in five movements and two 'parts') as somehow archetypal for Mahler[3] must take note of the fact that it was a developing archetype: evolving conceptually towards an ever clearer hierarchical arrangement of 'purely musical' movements. As a whole, the radical or revolutionary Third[4] could thus also be interpreted as seeking more conservatively to frame dynamic Darwinian evolution (both in Nature and in Society) as an eternal or inevitable organic structure. On this reading, the vulgar riot of the personified forces of Nature in the first movement is tamed in a musical procession that has minuetting flowers and clog-dancing animals properly subordinated to the 'noble Adagio', the 'higher form' that smiled down upon them all like the Emperor himself. Does the larger form therefore validate the aesthetic absolutism and progressively recreate the *status quo* that the symphony's localized musical manners seemed to challenge?

Meaning and the reinterpretation of form

The ambivalence of the Third in this respect – celebrating Mahler's dominion over the forms of his culture in a way that appeared to threaten it (and them) – necessitates still closer consideration of his idiosyncratic kind of programmaticism. An important aspect of the evolutionary relationship with the Second Symphony may be usefully examined by comparing the closely related third movements of the two works. Each is a large-scale Scherzo with contrasting Trio. The first-section material of both movements is derived from an existing song, while the Trio melody is a new element that is dramatically opposed to the Scherzo material and generates increasing tension. This erupts in a culminatory explosion, or 'Durchbruch' in Adorno's term, in which a quite other kind of music makes a startling appearance before the movement concludes with the returned Scherzo material. The similarities further extend to the fact that in both cases interpretation on the basis of the source song-text was elaborated by Mahler in one or more private 'programmatic' explanations.

It is important to stress Adorno's observation that Mahler's many settings from *Des Knaben Wunderhorn* (his sole source of song-texts from around 1887 to 1899) do not share the subjective lyrical manner of most other song-writing of the period.[5] They rather present objective metaphors constructed out of contrasted, juxtaposed and superimposed kinds of 'characteristic' music in which symphonic argument is frequently present in embryo. Mahler himself explained how they work while talking to Natalie Bauer-Lechner about the song *Das irdische Leben* ('Earthly Life'). He begins with a significant echo of Nietzsche's discussion of the *Wunderhorn* poems:

> ... with songs ... you can express so much more in the music than the words directly say. The text is actually a mere indication of the deeper significance to be extracted from it, of concealed treasure.
>
> In this way, I feel that human life (in the poem to which I give the interpretative title 'Das irdische Leben') is symbolized by the child's crying for bread and the answer of the mother, consoling it with promises again and again. In life, everything that one most needs for the growth of spirit and body is withheld until – as with the dead child – it is too late. And I believe that this is characteristically and frighteningly expressed in the uncanny notes of the accompaniment which bluster past as in a storm, in the child's anguished cry of fear and the slow monotonous responses of the mother – of Fate, which is in no particular hurry to satisfy our cries for bread.[6]

Nothing in this song, perhaps nothing in Mahler, is simply 'music'. Everything speaks, signifies and attempts to justify itself as an image or an expressive gesture, no matter if ordained by formal convention. Even the accompaniment figuration is interpreted as an image of 'fate', in which the human voice, both crying *and* consoling, is helplessly enfolded. In the outwardly more humorous content of 'St Anthony of Padua's Sermon to the Fishes', out of which the Second Symphony's C minor Scherzo was fashioned, the figuration that propels the music forward is personified: it depicts the mindless fish who fail to heed the preacher and continue in their selfishly

fishy ways in spite of his sermon. Mahler subsequently interpreted the climactic catastrophe (eight bars after cue 50) as 'an outburst of despair' on the
part of the symphonic protagonist, for whom 'the world and life become
chaotic nightmare'.[7] On another occasion, and still more revealingly, he would
describe the 'fish' music of the Second's Scherzo as representative of 'the
incomprehensible bustle of life' – an image of social pleasure from which the
composer-subject is significantly excluded. The music therefore 'seems *eerie*,
like the milling of dancing figures in a brightly lit ballroom, into which you
look from the dark night outside – from such a *distance* that you can *not* hear
the *music* any more! Life becomes senseless to you, a horrible nightmare
[Spuk] which you may perhaps run from with a cry of disgust – this is the
3rd movement'.[8]

The dancing folk out of whose 'natural' merriment symphonic scherzos
(like that of Mahler's First) had been fashioned for over half a century do not
come off too well here. How right Bekker was to point out that in the Third's
scherzo, the initial material, with its eventually reassumed, 'coarse', peasant-
dance associations, is also characterized as the music of *animals* – for whose
ultimate dispatch Mahler seems now to enlist the help of Nature herself,
conceived as a force of revolutionary self-transcendence. But we must listen
carefully to the music of the Trio's corny 'philosophical posthorn' and the
ensuing outburst (cue 31) – which here has so strikingly tangible an effect on
the dancing animals, who no longer return as 'fate', but go rushing off in a
festival of anarchic violence. The ancient form of scherzo and trio, its inher-
ited 'naturalness' already reinterpreted as an image of repressive symmetry,
becomes a frame for edgy caricature. The animals of the Third's scherzo
have bigger ears than the fish of the Second and seem to *listen* to the
posthorn tune, but fail to understand with a wilfulness that goes far beyond
what Tradition demands.

Here we encounter the darker side of the ironic 'humour' which Mahler
would speak of in connection with this movement, and with other parts of
the Third Symphony; the darkness that reflects Schopenhauer's view of the
world as 'the battleground of tormented and agonized beings who continue to
exist only by each devouring the other'.[9] This was the chaotic world of Will
whose nature (in every sense) was a cycle of inevitably unsatisfied desires in
which 'the subject of willing is constantly lying on the revolving wheel of
Ixion'.[10] For Schopenhauer only the world-renouncing contemplative artist
could halt that wheel; perhaps, indeed, in a great Adagio of the kind where,
as Mahler explained to Natalie Bauer-Lechner shortly after completing the
Third in August 1896, 'everything is resolved into quiet "being"; the Ixion-

wheel of appearances has at last been brought to a standstill ... So, contrary to custom – and without knowing why at the time – I concluded my Second and Third Symphonies with Adagios: that is, with a higher as opposed to a lower form.'[11]

The *composition* of the Third Symphony, however, had ended not with the Adagio (written in 1895), but the gigantic first movement (1896) in which noble Schopenhauerian quietism is replaced with the iconoclastic optimism of Nietzsche's *Die fröhliche Wissenschaft*, written, as the philosopher stated in his preface to the second edition, 'in the language of the wind that thaws ice and snow: high spirits, unrest, contradiction and April weather are present in it, and one is instantly reminded no less of the proximity of winter than of the triumph over winter that is coming, must come, and perhaps already has come.'[12] Mahler's descriptions of *this* movement, as we shall see, were as Nietzschean as could be, for all that he would wish in 1901 to reject 'the whole deceitful and viciously shameless immorality of Nietzsche's superiority of an elite'.[13] The socialist-modernist spirit of the 1880s seems, after all, to re-emerge as a deeper pretext for his symbolic reinterpretations of form, however contradictory the signs and signals that surround, and indeed resound in the Third Symphony.

The evolving conception

'It's the best and most mature of my works. With it I shall conclude my "Passion Trilogy".'

Mahler on the Third (to Annie Sommerfeld) in 1896[14]

In 1893, Mahler claimed that his first two symphonies (although the Second was not yet completed) contained the 'inner aspect' of his whole life ('I have written into them, in my own blood, everything that I have experienced and endured').[15] By contrast, the Third was conceived from the start as a cheerful and even humorous affair. It was to celebrate the 'happy life' that the Second had inaugurated after dispelling apocalyptic horrors with its concluding choral hymn to the individual spirit. Certainly the first known plans for the Third, quoted in slightly different forms by both Alma Mahler and Paul Bekker[16] (no original source has survived), suggest that the tormented 'Wayfarer' of old was now ready to submit to the innocent loveliness of the world that the birds and flowers had once fruitlessly invited him to enjoy.[17]

What was apparently the earliest of these lists of movement-titles runs as follows in Bekker's version:

> The Happy Life [*Das glückliche Leben*], a summer-night's dream (not after Shakespeare ... reviewer's notes).
>
> I. What the forest tells me
> II. What the twilight tells me
> III. What love tells me
> III. What the twilight tells me
> IV. What the flowers in the meadow tell me
> V. What the cuckoo tells me
> VI. What the child tells me

Interestingly, this plan is already for a six-movement symphony (with uncertainty over the order of movements II and III) – or rather a suite of what look like post-Schumannesque Romantic nature-pieces. Their titles evoke the expressive world of the first movement of the First Symphony and are cast in studiedly 'naive' form, culminating explicitly in a *child's* vision. No conflict-laden drama on the scale of the Second is indicated here. All the movements, with the possible exception of 'What love tells me', were apparently to be characteristic genre-studies. More than anything, the plan suggests that Mahler was at this time envisaging a sort of 'Pastoral Symphony' of his own, celebrating the natural world as it was seen in dreams by the early Romantics and the compilers of the *Wunderhorn* anthology.

Of an inner programme, linking and justifying this sequence of movements, little can be surmised. We might, however, note how the first and last groups of three movements seem to form units. The last, apparently a light and humorous procession of flowers, cuckoos and children, contrasts somewhat with the first group, where the serious business of love is preceded by tales of the twilight and the forest. If there seems little indication of a subject in this first group that would merit full-scale symphonic treatment, we should at least remember that the forest was the place where the Romantic poet typically experienced the mysterious duality of the world in sharpest definition: where the Black Hunter lurked unseen behind an idyllic tableau of animals scurrying beneath slanting sun-beams, to the sound of far-off hunting-horns; the green depths where by night the beating hooves of Goethe's *Erlkönig* echoed amidst the screeches of nocturnal predators.

There are no sure grounds on which to date any plans for the Third earlier than the summer of 1895. The roots of the idea could nevertheless reach back as far as 1892, when Mahler was embarking upon a major batch of

Wunderhorn settings (*Das himmlische Leben* was to be composed in February) towards the end of the long interim period in work on the Second Symphony. In April that year, Mahler wrote to his sister Justine about the *Wunderhorn* 'humour' as he saw it – humour 'in the best and truest sense of the word, something for which only a few exceptional men are created'.[18] The ironic cuckoo-song *Ablösung im Sommer*, which would form the basis of the Third's scherzo, had certainly been composed by this time.

Of the second of the two early plans, rather more can perhaps be said. Its closer approximation to the final version suggests that it post-dates the 'Happy Life' draft. For we now find added the title, and some interesting details, of a newly conceived 'introduction', whose relationship to the first movement of the work as we know it can at once be recognized:

I.   Summer marches in (Fanfare – cheerful [lustiger] march – Introduction
       with wind and concertante double-basses only)
II. What the forest tells me (lst movement)
III. What love tells me (Adagio)
IV. What the twilight tells me (Scherzo, strings only)
V.   What the flowers in the meadow tell me
VI. What the cuckoo tells me
VII. What the child tells me[19]

We can again, of course, only hypothesize as to the date of this plan. The earliest I would want to suggest would be the summer of 1893. It is a more serious draft than the first, and might have been related to some musical sketches. Although the subsequent first movement was finally composed only in the summer of 1896, *after* the other movements of the symphony, it is also apparent that the few sketched bars that Mahler himself seems to have regarded as the 'seed' from which the rest of the work grew all relate to material that was to find its way into the first movement.[20] Prominent on the page is music that could well merit the description 'cheerful march' and was to feature significantly in the completed first movement (Ex.1, Plate 1, and Appendix II). These inked sketches (and the page they are on has in fact been dated '1893 Steinbach' by some unknown hand) were given to Natalie Bauer-Lechner by Mahler in 1896, but occupy only the first side of a double sheet of manuscript-paper – the other three sides all bearing sketches (mostly in pencil) of *Second* Symphony material, in particular part of that work's Andante, which we know Mahler completed in the summer of 1893. Given that this was the first summer at Steinbach, and that Mahler was to have the famous little composing-house built for the following year,[21] it is tempting to

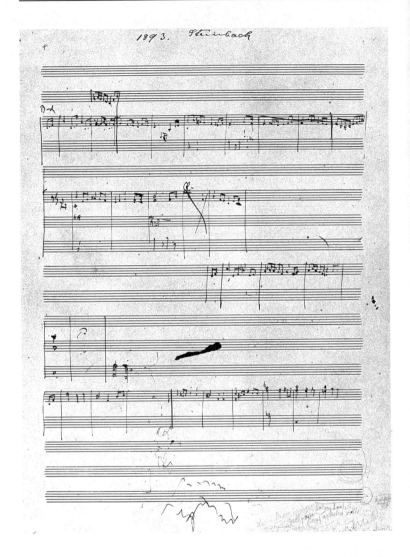

Plate 1 The sketch page bearing what may be the earliest notated ideas for the Third Symphony (first movement). Mahler gave it, with others, to Natalie Bauer-Lechner in 1896; it was probably she who dated it '1893 Steinbach'. (Reproduced by permission of Stanford University Libraries: Memorial Library of Music 630, Department of Special Collections.)

decipher faint pencil jottings at the foot of the first Third Symphony sketch-page as relating in part to the directions he would give the local builder. In one area the words 'Idyllisch' and 'arbeiten wollte' ['wanted to work'] can be made out, later 'Auf dem See [On the lake] Ver ... [?] Ludwig ... [?] Fensterhöhlen [window cavities/recesses] ... [?]'.

Example 1

Here, perhaps, is evidence of the real inception-point of the Third Symphony, post-dating by perhaps only a very short time the rounding-out of the conception of the Second (and the dawning realization of the kind of answer he sought to the first movement's questions). There is as yet, how-ever, no sign in this plan of the Nietzsche setting (later variously entitled 'What night tells me' – an early draft is curiously headed 'Nro 3' – and 'What man tells me'). Perhaps he had not completed the reading of *Also sprach Zarathustra* and *Die fröhliche Wissenschaft* that was ultimately to facil-itate the decisive re-focussing of the whole scheme, accommodating in a most fruitful way his vision of a work that was always intended to celebrate Nature as seen through the eyes of a *Wunderhorn* child. This was the case even before the *himmlische Leben* song had become involved. How interesting it is to find that the first movement Mahler appears to have begun drafting, once he had installed himself in his small lakeside studio in June 1895 (Plate 2), was the subsequent 'flowers' minuet (no. 2 in the final version), but under the heading *'Was das Kind erzählt'* ('What the child tells').[22]

This fact, coupled with the dual numbering in the above plan (II being also described as '1. Satz', which would set all the other numbering back by one), possibly accounts for an 1895 manuscript of the full draft of the move-ment having continued to bear the number '6', even though its title had been changed to the final *Was mir die Blumen auf der Wiese erzählen*.[23] For by that time it was the 1892 *Wunderhorn* setting *Das himmlische Leben* that had taken over the 'Child' title, and also (at least by the end of August 1895) the culminatory position which that title had always been accorded in the plans.

Amongst the other movement titles common to both early plans, 'What love tells me', described in the second as 'Adagio', presents no problem of identification, remaining a permanent feature of all the plans and appearing in the symphony's final form. Only the forest, twilight and cuckoo movements remain somewhat enigmatic. For all that I have suggested about the possible role and content of the 'forest' movement, no draft with that title exists to indicate what its musical character might have been. Nevertheless, when the 'animals' scherzo makes its appearance in the scheme, it is specifically woodland or 'forest' animals that are invoked by the consistent title formula: *Was mir die Thiere* im Walde *erzählen* (my emphasis). Indeed, I

Plate 2 The Gasthof on the Attersee, Upper Austria, where Mahler composed the Third Symphony in the summers of 1895 and '96 in the small white studio to the right. The village of Steinbach (far right) and the Höllengebirge are visible in the background. The photograph was taken in the early 1930s. (Reproduced by permission of Samuel Schweizer.)

would suggest that this movement might be seen as an amalgamation of all *three* of these otherwise enigmatic ideas. Certainly the 1895 draft of the Scherzo was clearly entitled *'Was mir die Dämmerung erzählt'* before the last two words were scratched out and replaced with *'... Thiere im Walde erzählen'*.[24] And of course this is the movement that derives its initial material from Mahler's setting of the *Wunderhorn* poem *Ablösung* (the song being called *Ablösung im Sommer*), which skittishly describes the replacement of the spring cuckoo, fallen to its death, by the beguiling nightingale of summer. The song is even in essence a juxtaposition of lyrical 'nightingale' music and a perky little dance in which, surely, is imparted nothing so much as 'What the cuckoo tells me.'

Betraying the complexity of its pre-history, there is a bewildering array of numberings on the front page of this 1895 draft of the Scherzo ('Nro 2' scratched out in the top right-hand section of the page, a larger 'Nro 5' above the amended title, and a pencilled 'Nro 4' in the bottom left). This should, I think, be taken as a strong indication that it was still the second of the above plans that Mahler was working to in the summer of 1895. I say this because if one accepts that the draft of the subsequent 'flowers' minuet had in its *retitled* form (thus momentarily eliminating altogether the idea of a 'Child' movement) at some point been placed as the final movement in a sequence that can be reckoned as either six or seven in total (depending upon whether the first two movements are seen as separate or an introduction/first-movement unit), then all the above-mentioned numberings on the Scherzo draft can be understood: if, as I have suggested, we see it as having drawn into itself elements of all three of the original 'forest', 'twilight' and 'cuckoo' conceptions.

The problem may well have remained that of the underlying programmatic conception which might explain the sequence of movements. Its final clarification seems to have resolved a confusion in Mahler's mind between the original idea of the 'humorous' suite of nature-pieces and the grand conception, vaster even than that of the Second Symphony, which was growing almost of its own accord as, in the summer of 1895, he drafted the movements from no. 2 onwards, although without a clear sense of their final order. That Nietzsche played a significant part in the solution is indicated by the title appended to the new scheme that Mahler excitedly announced to Arnold Berliner in a letter from Steinbach of 17 August, 1895, and subsequently to Fritz Löhr on 29 August.[25] Here is the plan as included with the letter to Löhr, on a separate quarto sheet:

Symphony No. III
'THE GAY SCIENCE' [*DIE FRÖHLICHE WISSENSCHAFT*]
A summer morning's dream

I.   Summer marches in.
II. What the flowers in the meadow tell me.
III. What the animals in the forest tell me.
IV. What night tells me. (Alto solo).
V. What the morning bells tell me. (Women's chorus with alto solo).
VI. What love tells me.
     Motto: 'Father look upon my wounds!
        Let no being be lost!'
     (From the *Knaben Wunderhorn*)
VII. Heavenly life [*Das himmlische Leben*]. (Soprano solo, humorous).

Although the dream was in 1896 to be allotted specifically to a Nietzschean 'noon-day' (*Mittagstraum*),[26] it has here moved from the Shakespearean-sounding 'summer night' of the first plan to the time of day when Mahler himself was habitually at his most productive during the summer. And it all bears the title of Nietzsche's book, from whose poetic sequel, *Also sprach Zarathustra*, the (as yet undisclosed) text of the fourth movement was to be taken.

In his important study of Mahler's musical semantic and his literary influences, Constantin Floros has in fact played down the role of Nietzsche and suggested that the final programmatic format of the Third bears richer comparison with two poems from Siegfried Lipiner's *Buch der Freude* of 1880.[27] The poems in question, 'Genesis' (a dream-vision of the Creation) and 'Hymne', are not, however, referred to in any of Mahler's explanations of the work, nor directly quoted in the manuscript superscriptions in the final version. Other poetic 'sources' that he did refer to (like the Second Part of Goethe's *Faust* and Hölderlin's poem 'The Rhine')[28] must surely be given equal weight in any consideration of the literary roots and affinities of Mahler's metaphorical descriptions of the music, particularly of the first movement of the Third. But none even of these sources was accorded the high honour of direct and explicit inclusion in the plans for the Third, as the two works of Nietzsche certainly were. Indeed Lipiner's influence on it may well have been primarily through conversations about Nietzsche which Mahler had with him. One thing is clear: the conception of the work that had emerged in August 1895 bears little sign of Schopenhauerian or Wagnerian 'renunciation'.

The final 'chain of being' conception is not made explicit here, but that Mahler already saw it as logically implied by this plan is evident from the vital letter which accompanied the above sheet, where he elaborated on it as follows:

> The emphasis on my *personal* emotional life (in the form of what things tell *me*) is appropriate to the work's singular intellectual content. II–IV *incl.* are to express the *successive orders* of being, which I shall correspondingly express thus
>
> II. W[hat] t[he] *flowers* t[ell] m[e].
> III. What the *animals* tell me.
> IV. What the *night* tells me (*man*).
> V. What the *morning bells* tell me (*the angels*)
> last two numbers with *text* and song.
> VI. What *love* tells me, is a synopsis of my feelings
> towards *all beings*, in which *deeply painful* spiritual
> paths are not avoided, but gradually lead through to a
> *blessed faith* [*selige Zuversicht*]: 'die *fröhliche*
> Wissenschaft'. Finally *Das himmlische Leben* (VII),
> which I have now, however, finally called
> '*What the child tells me*'.
>
> No. I, *Summer marches in*, should indicate the humorously subjective content. Summer is thought of as a *victor* – embracing everything that *grows and blossoms, crawls and runs, thinks and desires* and finally *what we have intuition of* [*ahnen*]. (Angels – bells – transcendental).
>
> Over and above it all, *eternal love* acts within us – as the rays come together in a focal point. Do you understand now?[29]

The major additions made here are the bracketed glosses to the titles of movement 4 ('man') and movement 5 ('the angels') and the retitling of *Das himmlische Leben*. The central movements are now clearly arranged to 'express the successive orders of being'. In the following summer the image of 'mountain-rocks' was even to be attached to the first movement's newly separated 'introduction'[30] (soon re-named 'Pan sleeps'), while Mahler was to write of the 'love' Adagio to Anna von Mildenburg: 'I could almost call this movement "What God tells me"!'[31] — thus extending the chain logically through all but the eventually discarded 'child' movement. Still more interesting here, perhaps, are the comments on the nature of the expressive manner to be employed, indicating that Mahler fully understood both the history and full import of Nietzsche's assertion in *Die fröhliche Wissenschaft* that 'whatever in nature and history is of my own kind, speaks to me ... We are always only in our own company.'[32]

We have seen that the range of musical-stylistic metaphors employed by Mahler not only reflects and makes audible human 'nature', but creates a metaphor for human society: including both the elegant gracefulness of the flowers and the peasant charm, even 'coarseness', of the dancing animals.[33] Perhaps, indeed, such a world *could* be imaginatively 'held together' in bourgeois culture only by the child, for all its shamelessly self-centred amorality – the child who for Nietzsche came to represent 'innocence and forgetfulness, a sport, a self-propelling wheel, a first motion, a sacred Yes'.[34] A significant turning-point in *Also sprach Zarathustra* is marked by Zarathustra's account, in 'The Prophet' (Part II), of his dream of having become a Schopenhauerian ascetic, locking himself up in a 'lonely hill-fortress of death', until there come three thunderous blows on the door. Zarathustra cannot open it, but it finally gives way of its own accord, torn open by a 'raging wind' that tosses a black coffin into the mausoleum:

> And in the roaring and whistling and shrilling, the coffin burst asunder and vomited forth a thousand peals of laughter.
> And from a thousand masks of children, angels, owls, fools and child-sized butterflies it laughed and mocked and roared at me.[35]

It was one of Mahler's great imaginative achievements to draw the Third Symphony together out of what must have been a deep intuitive understanding of the significance of that passage in Nietzsche, in which Schopenhauerian pessimism was finally dispelled by wind-born laughter that was at once foolish, childlike and angelic; the laughter that set Zarathustra on the path to becoming 'a child – an awakened one', who could tell the saint in the forest: 'I love mankind.'[36] As this childlike love was to be tested and explained to the full in the final Adagio, so is the manner of its occurrence to Zarathustra one of the keys to the first movement, whose title (even in this letter of 1895, when the movement was still only tentatively sketched) 'Summer marches in' was supposed to 'indicate the *humorously* subjective content' (my emphasis). It was a kind of humour that was clearly intended to serve and further, rather than deflate, the epic scheme of the work that had now evolved. In a conversation with Natalie Bauer-Lechner in July 1896, Mahler, having confessed to the 'deeply serious' nature of the Night and Love movements, bewailed the fact that a friend to whom he had played the work had disapproved of the Angels movement as being 'too slight after such profundity', and thus failed to grasp 'that the humour here has to aim at such heights of expression where all other means fall short.'[37]

It was in this Nietzschean humour that the secret of the symphony's deep seriousness lay – the seriousness with which it had now finally reverted to the scheme of the Second Symphony (see p.38) in order to build a stable architectural edifice in which to explore and extend the answer to the 'greatest questions of humanity' that he had fashioned there. In fact the questions as put had become irrelevant:

> For what can they signify in the totality of things, in which *everything lives*; will and *must* live? Can a spirit that has dwelt upon the eternal creation-thoughts of the deity in such a symphony as this die? No, one grows confident that everything is eternally and unalterably born for the good. Even human sorrow and distress has no place here any more. The most sublime cheerfulness [*Heiterkeit*] prevails, an eternally radiant day – for gods, to be sure, not men, for whom it is the great and terrible Unknown, something eternally ungraspable ... I shall style the first movement ' Part I' and will then have a long pause. But I now want to call the whole thing 'Pan, Symphonic Poems'.[38]

The release of the Dionysian forces of Nature as described in Nietzsche's *The Birth of Tragedy* had become possible in the first movement – whose march would in 1896 gain the subtitle 'Bacchic procession' – only, Mahler said, through the courage he had gained by first composing all the other movements.[39] But the surprising length and nature of that movement also, as he began to realize, destabilized the structure and threatened the 'symphony' itself, just as the Bacchantes and Maenads of Dionysus had threatened the society of Cadmus' Thebes in Euripides' play *The Bacchae* (which Mahler knew) and torn its king, Pentheus, to pieces. For all that it was an outcome of the others, and modelled closely upon the march-dominated finale as developed in the previous two symphonies, he never considered placing the movement anywhere other than at the beginning of the work. The *himmlische Leben* song of 1892 had become superfluous and confusing as a conclusion. Mahler's developing conception had drawn it into the symphony as, in a sense, musically generative *of* some of it (he even experimented with prominent quotation of its material in the first movement's march in a sketch in 1895, while retaining more fleeting allusions in the second movement).[40] It might equally well have been used as a preludial epigraph. A whole other symphony would eventually be composed to accommodate it and conclude the 'Tetralogie'[41] of the first four symphonies. But their climax was to remain the Adagio of the Third, a Nietzschean reading of which Mahler nevertheless hinted at in a letter of November 1896 to Annie Mincieux, where he described it as 'the highest level of the structure: God! or, if you like, the *Übermensch.*'[42]

Music as metaphor here gave way to pure, 'higher' form not simply as received mystery, but also as animated lyrical expression in the first person. For an explanation, and the beginnings of an interpretative key to the expressive content of that Adagio, we might return to *Die fröhliche Wissenschaft*. In a section called 'The "Humanness" of the Future', Nietzsche explains what must be endured and surmounted by the *Übermensch*, for whom – externally and metaphysically – 'God is dead':[43]

> if one could burden one's soul with all of this – the oldest, the newest, losses, hopes, conquests, and the victories of humanity; if one could finally contain all this in one soul and crowd it into a single feeling – this would surely have to result in a happiness that humanity has not known so far: the happiness of a god full of power and love, full of tears and laughter, a happiness that, like the sun in the evening continually bestows its inexhaustible riches, pouring them into the sea, feeling richest, as the sun does, only when the poorest fisherman is still rowing with golden oars! This godlike feeling would then be called – humanness.[44]

The divine, higher love of the Adagio need suggest no capitulation to religious faith, but rather a subsuming of Christian 'suffering' in a Nietzschean process of becoming, if now explicitly on the level of individual consciousness.

4

The music

The positive vision of the Third Symphony proved harder and harder for Mahler to sustain in subsequent years. It was as if, after they had been 'explained' and conceptually reconciled, the disruptive forces to which his music gave such startling expression were to continue to develop energies and strategies of their own. It is his attempt and desire to master them that makes Mahler both modern and anti-modern in a way that commends him so forcefully to our own time: not as some 'transitional' curiosity, but the summit and watershed between heroic Romanticism and truth-scarred Modernism. The conflict between those two impulses would lead him ever more compellingly back to the Adagio manner of troubled inwardness, yet the achieved balance and hope of the Third and Eighth Symphonies are as important a part of his legacy as the more tragic Sixth; as the last movement of *Das Lied von der Erde* or the shadowy, sepulchral E's that conclude *Das himmlische Leben* and the Fourth Symphony (as once they might have concluded the Third).

It will prove useful, in considering the music of the Third, to leave the last-composed first movement until the end, and begin, as Mahler himself seems to have done in the summer of 1895, with the movements of the 'Second Part' of the symphony. Paul Bekker points out that not only did Mahler require a long pause between the first and second movements; in his own performances he sought to position the concert-interval at that point.[1] Extending Mahler's own observation that the later movements follow the first 'on quite a different plane',[2] Bekker cleverly observed that whereas the first part of the symphony was about Becoming, the second part deals with what is; with *what has become*.[3]

Movement 2 *Tempo di Menuetto/Grazioso* 'What the flowers in the meadow tell me'

Amongst his many pioneering observations in 1921, Bekker was to suggest that comparison with the Second Symphony was as valuable here as in the case of the third movement.[4] The Andante of the Second (also *grazioso*) was in the same A-B-A-B-A form that this movement adopts, and both engage in a curious, anachronistic mixture of minuet and scherzo. In each case the minuet material has the character of a relaxed and contrasting 'trio' to the proto-scherzo material, but is nonetheless given formal precedence as the primary mode of the movement. What results is another version of the Mahlerian structure that deliberately threatens its own stability.

In a dramatically evolving symphonic type whose argument was fully engaged only in the first and final movements, Mahler had come to regard the internal movements of the old symphonic suite as comprising an 'interlude'[5] which was outside the engaged present-tense of its dramatic narration. With the Third, however, Mahler conceptually or 'programmatically' justified the complete succession of unequally weighted movements. Consequently, the A major 'flowers' minuet was able, as he put it, to become 'the most carefree thing that I have ever written – as carefree as only flowers are. It all sways and waves in the air, as light and graceful as can be, unaffected by any gravitational pull from the depths, like flowers bending on their stems in the wind.'[6] The imagery is aptly chosen, for although the relative-minor-orientated 'B'-section material (cue 3) once again cuts some odd capers and seems intent upon a developmental life of its own, the graceful minuet is prepared to surprise us with a coquettish smile when it returns (e.g. cue 6), half-way through its first phrase, perfectly in command of the movement and its formal necessities. The final point of 'return', at the start of the coda (cue 14), is particularly striking. The second and more developmental 'B'-section has found its way into A *flat* major and a purposeful little solo-violin variation of its central motif which, like some absent-minded bee, is busy describing a decorated descending scale of A flat major when it suddenly finds that it has slipped unsuspectingly into the mouth of the voluptuous flower in E major (and in $\frac{3}{4}$) that had been waiting there all the time (Ex. 2).

Mahler was soon to discover, however, that this was one of the many startling details in this movement that were lost upon the audiences who first heard it out of context. They surprised both him and themselves by finding it wholly unshocking and charming. Mahler did not like the idea of being regarded 'a "meditative", finespun "singer of nature"': I always feel it strange that when most people speak of "Nature" what they mean is flowers, little birds, the woodland scents etc. No one knows the god Dionysus, or great Pan.'[7] Nevertheless, the minuet itself *is* at first apparently all charm and smiles, the main theme sitting demurely within the regular metre. It is barely tickled by the F sharp minor counter-theme (bars 19ff) whose triplet figuration harbours little of the threat of that in the Second's Andante. Its climax comes shortly thereafter (bars 27-30) with a richly blossoming lyrical gesture that seems to want to cadence in D major (the key in which the symphony will conclude) – although in proper Schopenhauerian fashion its desire is not really satisfied (Ex. 3). But it is coaxed back into A major for a final paragraph which emphasizes its symmetrical, 'closing' purpose.

For all that, the 'B'-section material leaps eagerly into action the moment the final cadence has been reached. Whereas the minuet ('A') is presented in a closed 'a-b-a' unit, the new F sharp minor music stresses its contrasting, developmental nature by describing a kind of 'a-b-*c*' form and creating a quite new kind of texture: reiterated staccato triads accompanying a faster dance in $\frac{3}{8}$ (corresponding to the triplets of the preceding section) whose first phrase is oddly nine bars long. Excited violin quintuplets lead into its second part, a still more purposeful and energetic dance in $\frac{2}{4}$ (derived from the minuet material and appropriately marked 'Zigeuner' ('gypsy') by Willem Mengelberg in his conducting-score of the symphony). This in *its* turn gives way to the fastest music in the movement: a *perpetuum mobile* chain of whirling semiquavers, again accompanied by vamped staccato triads, in $\frac{9}{8}$. Initially in E minor, the passage is marked by a change of key-signature to E major, which is firmly reached as the music, speeding up even more (*'Etwas drängender'*), tumbles into a highly significant quotation of material from the song that usurped this movement's original title before being removed from the scheme of the symphony altogether: the 'child's' song *Das himmlische Leben*. The music alluded to is the accompaniment to the phrase 'wir hüpfen und singen' (see bars 31ff) and the subsequent account of St Peter's obliging fishing expedition (bars 101ff; see Ex. 4).[8]

The dancing momentum of that song, growing as it does out of a kind of lullaby, is one of Mahler's most potent images of a temporal progression that is intentionally 'all-encompassing', just as that of its companion-piece (*Das irdische Leben*) we know to have been all-denying. It may not bring 'great Pan' back into the picture here, but it certainly reinforces the protean potential of this 'scherzo'-like foil to the gentle minuet, and perhaps explains Mahler's continuing description of the movement to Natalie Bauer-Lechner: 'As you might imagine, the mood doesn't remain one of innocent, flower-like serenity, but suddenly becomes serious and oppressive. A stormy wind blows across the meadow and shakes the leaves and blossoms, which groan and whimper on their stems, as if imploring release into a higher realm.'[9]

It would not be difficult to apply this to the movement's closing section, following the somewhat more extended and wayward repetition of the 'B'-

Example 2 *(cont. next page)*

Example 2

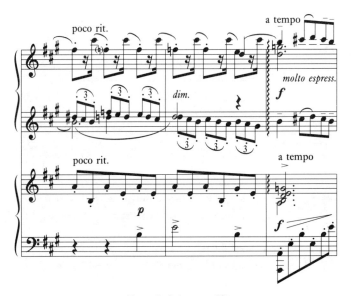

Example 3 *(cont. p. 58)*

Example 3

Example 4

section with, once more, its allusion to *Das himmlische Leben*. Here the closed 'a-b-a' form of the minuet material is charmingly emphasized: first by its extended and lushly decorated version of the blossoming, D-major-tending gesture and then, the proliferating string decoration continuing, by a wilting 'Abgesang'. Its final, ravishingly Tristanesque elaboration, floated on the dominant preparation for the last four bars of A major, could well be taken as a brief expression of longing for higher things before 'nature' here runs its course and this 'smallest and most "inarticulate" '[10] of the work's movements ends precisely where and as it should.

Movement 3. *Comodo, Scherzando [Rondo]*. 'What the animals in the forest tell me'

'The scherzo especially, the animal-piece, is at once the most scurrilous and most tragic there ever was – in the way that only music can mystically lead us from the one to the other in the twinkling of an eye. The piece is really a sort of face-pulling and tongue-poking on the part of all Nature. But there is such a gruesome, Panic humour in it that one is more likely to be overcome by horror than laughter.'

Mahler on the Scherzo in 1899[11]

Having commented on the broader relationship between this movement and its counterpart in the Second Symphony, we might begin here by considering the song from which its primary material is derived. Bars 1-67 (one before cue 4) are an orchestral transcription, with only minor adjustments, of Mahler's *Wunderhorn* setting *Ablösung im sommer* ('Change-over in summer'), first published in the third volume of *Lieder und Gesänge* in 1892. Its text, including the repetitions and embellishments characteristically added by Mahler, has been translated as follows (the German of Arnim and Brentano's *Wunderhorn* original only – 'Ablösung' – is given alongside):[12]

Kuckuck hat sich zu Tod gefallen	Cuckoo has fallen to its death,
an einer holen Weiden	Fallen to its death on a green willow!
	Willow! Willow!
	Cuckoo is dead! Cuckoo is dead!
	Has fallen to its death!
Wer soll uns diesen Sommer lang	Who then shall all summer long
die Zeit und Weil' vertreiben	Beguile the time for us?
	Cuckoo! Cuckoo!
Ei, das soll tun Frau Nachtigall,	Oh, let it be Madame Nightingale!

Die sitzt auf grünem Zweige,	She sits on a green branch!
	The little, fine nightingale!
Sie singt und springt, ist allzeit froh,	She sings and springs, is always gay,
Wenn andre Vögel schweigen,	When other birds are silent!
	We wait for Madame Nightingale,
	She lives in the green glen,
	And when the cuckoo's call has stopped,
	Then she begins to sing!

By comparison with the 'St Anthony of Padua' song, this text appears surprisingly devoid of symbolic potential and would seem more likely to commend itself to a 'finespun "singer of Nature"' than a Dionysian mystic. The puzzle is, if anything, complicated still further by Mahler's setting of it, although the direction 'Mit Humor' provides the key.

Example 5

The cuckoo's fate inspires a grotesque little minor-key dance with a dry, wry vocal line, whose caricatured weeping on the thrice-repeated word 'willow' suggests that the singer's sad face is ironically painted on, like a clown's (Ex. 5). Its tendency to dispense with the third at cadences heightens the acerbity of this 'cuckoo' music and, indeed, of the contrast between it and the mellifluous stream of semiquavers in the tonic major which greets the nightingale after a double bar (for all the persistence of the sprightly staccato bass). This is the 'change-over', which is charmingly reflected in the music's now more properly Schubertian pastoral manner — until the return to the 'cuckoo' material in the last four lines prompts one of Mahler's most disconcerting pieces of musical symmetry. The key-signature changes back to the minor and the pianist pounds out a version of the last eight bars of the 'cuckoo' song. A soft variant of the naive opening dance-motto then concludes with an unexpectedly stark, *fortissimo* tonic chord — without the third. Certainly this could be construed as a kind of tongue-poking ... but of 'all Nature'? Are we again to read this prototypical *perpetuum-mobile* dance as a symbol of 'fate', apparently unconcerned whether the dead cuckoo is a foil for the comfortingly live nightingale that succeeds it, or vice versa; as a temporal extension of the Schubertian ambivalence between major and minor which will one day generate the mighty tragedy of the Sixth Symphony?

Clearly we are on the track of a conception which might link scurrilous humour with tragedy, although the transcription of the song as the opening section of the symphonic movement seems deliberately to soften and even prettify it: heightening its 'scherzando' charm and turning it into an apparently cohesive musical paragraph describing rather friendly animals prodding, rustling and fluttering through the forest twilight with nothing much in mind. They are sufficiently anthropomorphized to be associated with the genial peasants of the first Symphony's scherzo as well as the mocking and parodistic beasts of its *Todtenmarsch in Callots Manier*. Mahler is, of course, simply setting up one element within the larger symphonic framework of contrasts and oppositions that he intends to work with. For the animals will undergo some significant changes of character as the movement progresses in a more elaborate version of the Minuet's A-B-A-B-A structure, where the 'B'-sections here are the posthorn episodes over which so much ink has been spilled. Before coming to them, however, we must be clear that Mahler described the movement as a *rondo*. It is the animals' music that returns at each juncture. As the previous one had belonged to the flowers, so this movement belongs to the animals, whatever the posthorn player may, or may not, cause them to do.

This is important, given what we know about Mahler's reading of the exasperating 'fish' music in the Second Symphony's scherzo. Do these animals, with their often rather folksy human faces, inspire Mahler's, and our, disgust? Or are we sufficiently enchanted by them to suffer it, if and when they turn nasty (accepting that it is 'in their nature' to be so)? Musically they slip from C major into C minor and back again with an ease that was presaged in the original song. But C major seems to gain the upper hand when, at cue 4, new, more explicitly rumbustious and indeed 'scherzando' material is introduced as a kind of middle section in the larger a-b-a unit that both establishes the 'rondo' character of the movement and encloses its first complete structural element. This energetic dance soon begins to reveal something of Mahler's larger symbolic strategy while at the same time validating Adorno's interpretation of the animal energies in this movement as more seriously threatening to the idealist composer and his hierarchical culture than those of the scorned fish in St Anthony's river. By bar 83 — still in the scherzo material's 'middle section' — the triplets that so often bode ill in Mahler begin to generate high trills and, soon, a succession of those strange, trilled descending chords that presage apocalypse in the Finale of the Second Symphony (thirteen bars after cue 3). As if suggesting that the animals can frighten *themselves*, these chords occasion nervous little warning-cries from the birds which will be heard again later. (Ex. 6). At this point in the movement the violent energies are calmed in an idyllic C major codetta before the extended developmental repeat of the initial song material; but here too the potential for violence is exploited, as at the end of the 'cuckoo' material, up to cue 9 (bars 170-5). Furthermore, in view of my earlier suggestion that the song had from the start a darker symbolic potential, it is surely significant that the 'nightingale' material should acquire a brief quotation of the starving child's entreaty from *Das irdische Leben* at cue 10 in the clarinets (Ex. 7).

A new motif, anticipating the rhythm of the posthorn to come, shortly imparts a nervous expectancy to the whole texture, which is fulfilled with the entry of a muted trumpet (periodically reinforced by another) and an extended, military-style signalling. It continues through the passage from cue 12 to cue 14, in which the 'animals' material is increasingly subdued and fragmented, disappearing altogether when the posthorn is heard, 'as if from

Example 6

Example 7

the far distance'.[13] Here the key-signature changes to F major for the first of the two 'trio'-like episodes at whose outset, on both occasions, Mahler had written in the manuscript[14] a descriptive heading: *Der Postillon!* ('The Postilion!'). The further bracketed directions, which appear in the printed score, had then originally read 'Like the melody of the posthorn', before the second definite article was made indefinite.

The conflict between the views of Adorno and Hans Eggebrecht about the posthorn is the effective subject of the latter's subtly detailed discussion of this movement.[15] For Adorno it was indeed banal, a musical *objet trouvé* as so many of the early critics had suggested, in their response to it as a *quotation* of the popular band item *Die Post im Walde* or whatever). Its 'scandalously risky' aspect is deliberately softened, suggested Adorno, and drawn into the world of the 'artistic' scherzo whose animals nevertheless 'shake their heads' over it.[16] For Eggebrecht, like Adorno, the posthorn stands for a realm Otherness in the movement, but is 'composed' with the greatest artfulness as an image of untroubled beauty — the movement enfolding the two 'worlds' of music in its larger representation of *Mahler's* world, which finds its own fulfilment in a new, synthetic 'coherence of statement'[17] whose collage-like quality anticipates twentieth-century modernist experimentation. Adorno, suggests Eggebrecht, misinterprets the music ideologically in his determination to 'socially decode' it as the expression of a deformed and broken society.[18]

The manuscript's internal heading proves provocatively interesting, given Ernst Decsey's subsequent account, not mentioned by Eggebrecht, of his suggestion that the posthorn should be interpreted in the light of Lenau's poem 'Gentle was that night in May.' Mahler had been amazed by his insight: 'That's precisely what I had in mind ... I was thinking of the same poem, the same mood – how did you know?'[19] The poem[20] is in fact called *Der Postillon* and describes the poet's journey by post-coach (something Mahler had experienced as a child)[21] through a beautiful spring night in the countryside. The postilion stops the coach in sight of a churchyard where, he tells the poet, an old friend lies buried – a former comrade who had blown the horn like no other. He always stops here to sound his own horn as a greeting and in memory of the other, dead postilion:

> And the horn's bright tone
> resounded from the mountains,
> as it the dead postilion
> joined in its songs –[22]

Could this be the explanation of the manuscript's headings and the accompanying directions in the score? Not only does the posthorn expressly play a 'tune'[23], but it is on all occasions directed to sound 'as if from the [far] distance' (at times 'getting nearer'). Could this also explain why the simple melody is indeed so artfully extended and improvised with such 'feeling' that it will later draw the listening animals into an anticipation of Mahler's most engaged Adagio manner? For a moment, there, the music seems to respond to the bass-drum's repeated reminder of the solemn, funereal inspiration for this song of man – who walks by therefore, not quite so 'calmly' as Mahler's originally publicized programme had apparently suggested.[24] The passage clearly marked *Wie Nachhorchend!* ('As if overheard') (cue 28) certainly suggests a moment of fragile empathy between the two worlds. Eggebrecht correctly notes that there is no sign of the animals 'shaking their heads' over the posthorn's melody.[25] But is it not rather a question of the posthorn colonizing and monopolizing the movement in these episodes and turning the animals' nocturnal forest into a humanly perceived idyll and elegy? What happens *after* the two episodes is of the greatest interest. The music on both occasions becomes instinct with a kind of nervousness, shading into fear. At the end of this first episode, the edgy quality of the scherzo material already interpolated at cue 16 is is made clearer by the change of key-signature to F minor at cue 17 and a passage marked 'With mysterious haste', where the anticipated return of the scherzo material is delayed by a 'tremolando am Steg' fixation on the already quoted motif from *Das irdische Leben* (specifically from bar 351, five after cue 17).

It is worth recalling here Schopenhauer's belief that animals 'peacefully and serenely enjoy every present moment ... the life of the animal is a continual present ... in contrast to the conduct of human beings which is withdrawn from the innocence of nature by the first appearance of the faculty of reason'.[26] The threat that man (in Mahler's description) represents to the life of the animals is not only physical; his consciousness of mortality will destroy their world of 'eternal present'– an idea which Mahler was to invoke in an early plan for the Fourth Symphony in which, significantly, both *Das himmlische Leben* and *Das irdische Leben* were to stress the conceptual relationship between children and animals in a somewhat anarchic heaven where they share an ironic and humorous view of adult human culture and its concerns.[27]

In the Third Symphony's scherzo, the 'irdische Leben' nerviness, once dispelled, is replaced by the central return of the animals' material, their charm and original key of C major (reached via F major) once more restored.

Their regained humour certainly acquires 'tongue-poking' characteristics, however. The directions for the various stages of the ever more boisterous dance move from *Lustig* ('jolly') through *Übermütig* ('high-spirited' or 'insolent') to *Grob!* ('coarse' or even 'gross') for the marvellous knees-up at cue 23. This again throws up apocalyptic images before the warning birds announce the final posthorn episode. After *that,* the briefly sympathetic, posthorn-imitating animals seem not so much nervous as ripe for hysteria and they quickly take flight towards the catastrophic outburst of cue 31. Here is Mahler's description of the movement's conclusion:

> Only at the end of the 'Animals' does there fall once more the heavy shadow of lifeless Nature, of still uncrystallized, inorganic matter, that is thrown over the conclusion of the introduction. But here it represents a relapse into lower forms of animal creation before the mighty leap towards consciousness [zum Geist] in the highest earthly creature, Man.[28]

We might even see in this shadow the silhouette of Pan himself. The great signal of the horns and trombones that blasts out above a tremolando chord of E flat minor (moving to D flat without the third) chills us to the marrow[29]. As if bent on realizing the full potential of the harsh conclusion of the little *Ablösung im Sommer* song, it seems to wish to remind the animals of their place in the scheme of things, and the symphony. This is no cry of disgust, as in the Second Symphony's scherzo, but a call to order – or, in human terms, *disorder,* celebrated now in the ensuing coda of brazen, almost barbaric splendour. The triumphant dancing oxen referred to by Adorno[30] seem to come stamping back into the picture, perhaps rudely mocking those more delicately sentient creatures who, like the flowers at the end of the second movement, had momentarily yearned for higher things. It might have been part of Mahler's purpose that we should not know whether to laugh or shudder at the yattering and clattering conclusion in C major. This scherzo does not seek to destroy itself, but rather, having won its own stability, rounds to threaten *us.*

Movement 4. *Sehr Langsam. Misterioso.* 'What Night tells me'
(Alto solo)

Movement 5. *Lustig im Tempo und keck im Ausdruck.* 'What the
angels/morning bells tell me' (women's and children's chorus
with alto solo)

Movement 6. (Finale) *Langsam. Ruhevoll. Empfunden.* 'What
Love tells me'

It is not simply for reasons of space that I discuss the last three movements
together. Mahler directs that they should follow on from each other without
breaks and, both musically and conceptually, they comprise a kind of 'third
part' to the symphony. The fourth movement also presents a significantly
new kind of beginning after unruly dionysian forces had seemed to push
Mahler, at the end of the scherzo, into the world of the as yet uncomposed
first movement. Like Wagner at the start of the *Ring* cycle, he recreates his
musical language from fundamental material: a primaeval whole-tone oscillation that is subsequently harmonized after the admonitory calls ('With mysterious expression') of the contralto, who gives voice to the accompanying
chords (F major–A minor, F sharp minor–A minor): 'Oh man! Oh man! ('O
Mensch!')

Mahler described this opening music as '... awakening from a confused
dream – or rather a gentle awakening to consciousness of one's own reality
[Sich-seiner-selbst-bewusst-werden]'.[31] As in Nietzsche's *Die fröhliche
Wissenschaft*', the dreamer wakes for a moment from the dream of 'being'
only to find that it must be resumed if all the contradictions of the world are
to be encompassed and held together – in Mahler's dream by a *Wunderhorn*
child, lost in a glitter of Christmas angels in the following movement. The
hope of eternal joy and the denying fatalism of 'woe' (and the philosophical
and religious systems that derive from it) are here presented as elemental
modes of human experience before being musically personified (as supplicant
and responding angels) in the reconciling fifth movement and then explored
to the full in the concluding Adagio.

Although Mahler deliberately avoids all the headier and more physical
manifestations of Zarathustra's 'joy' (which, perhaps, the previous movement
had momentarily glimpsed), his setting of the poem is a masterpiece of imaginative interpretation that concentrates on evoking the great stillness against
which Nietzsche has Zarathustra deliver it in the book: '... it grew more still
and mysterious, and everything listened [horchte], even the ass and

Zarathustra's animals of honour, the eagle and the serpent, likewise Zarathustra's cave and the great cool moon and the night itself.'[32] Mahler deliberately differentiates this song of solitary consciousness from the posthorn melody of the third movement. The 'expressive' features of the latter are here made into musical elements in their own right. Notated rubato and embellishment had there drawn out and confused the periodic character of the socially shared 'folksong'. The vocal line of the Night movement (whose even more subtly varying metrical notation caused Mahler some problems)[33] is paradoxically more of an 'arioso' which *tends towards* melody as the climactic, but also closing gesture of a beautifully turned and symmetrical musical structure. The symmetry is emphasized by Mahler's repetition of the opening *O Mensch!* (not in the Nietzsche), which divides the poem into two six-line stanzas and marks the beginning of the developing 'repetition' of the movement's opening section:

O Mensch! Gib Acht!	O man! Take heed!
Was spricht die tiefe Mitternacht?	What does the deep midnight say?
„Ich schlief, ich schlief –	I slept! I slept!
Aus tiefem Traum bin ich erwacht:–	I have awoken from deep dreaming!
Die Welt ist tief,	The world is deep!
Und tiefer als der Tag gedacht.	And deeper than the day conceives!
[O Mensch! O Mensch!]	O man! O man!
Tief ist ihr Weh –	Deep! Deep is its woe!
Lust – tiefer noch als Herzeleid;	Joy, joy deeper still than heart-ache!
Weh spricht;Vergeh!	Woe says: be lost!
Doch alle Lust will Ewigkeit –	But all joy wills eternity! –
– will tiefe, tiefe Ewigkeit!"	Wills deep, deep eternity![34]

The 'naturalness' of the musically expressed dichotomy between major and minor makes it no less painful for man, who would hold on to the aspiring melody of envisaged 'joy' while accepting the influential presence of 'woe' in the scheme of things. The musical harbinger of 'woe' is the mysterious rising-third motif, given three times to the oboe, once to the cor anglais, which deliberately signals the points in the movement at which D major darkens into D minor (roughly at the mid-point and end of each of the two, equal-length sections; the exact mid-point, in terms of bar numbers, occurs half way through bar 74). On the first and third occasions, as if to emphasize both its emblematic and onomatopaeic qualities, the motif is described in the score as being 'like a sound of nature' (*Wie ein Naturlaut*), but the final manuscript was more explicit. There, *all four* occurrences (bars 32, 44, 70 and 102) were clearly labelled *Der Vogel der Nacht!* ('The Bird of Night!'). Constantin Floros has suggested that the motif reproduces the cry of the tawny owl.[35] While I am inclined to agree with Eggebrecht, who prefers to regard this as a wholly symbolic bird,[36] it is interesting that the first appearance of the 'Midnight Song' in Nietzsche's book had followed a passage in which Zarathustra, who had been dancing in pursuit of Life, is momentarily halted by caves and thickets from which owls and bats fly up.[37] The manuscript label might still more convincingly be read as a reference to another poem, this time by Mahler's beloved Hölderlin.[38] Called 'Brevity' (*Die Kurze*), the second of its two stanzas runs:

> Like my joy is my song. – Who in the sundown's red
> Glow would happily bathe? Gone it is, cold the earth,
> And the bird of night [*der Vogel der Nacht*] whirrs
> Down, so close that you shield your eyes.

The presence of this non-human *Naturlaut* emphasizes the newly human-ized quality of those elements of the musical material which had themselves been 'sounds of Nature' long ago at the outset of the symphony's first move-ment. The initial 'mysterious' chords accompanying the soloist's *O Mensch* and the following harmonized version of the oscillating figure on the full complement of eight horns, not used in the second and third movements, were initially heard in bars 11–23 of the first. The main lyrical figure of the violins at cue 5 and following (compare the solo violin at cue 5 and the cul-minatory flowering of the vocal line at *Doch alle Lust will Ewigkeit!*, bar 119) had originally been an emphatic *ff* trumpet motif at bar 78 and following, up to cue 7. Such connections strongly emphasize the feeling of 'recommencing' a kind of third and final part of the symphony, for all that the composition of this movement preceded that of the first. Mahler himself even described the appearance of *O Mensch* in the first movement as being *from* the Night movement ('aus der "Nacht"'[39]) and would later claim that the material had even there been unconsciously cribbed from a composition of his school-days.[40]

The fifth movement, too, quotes earlier-composed material, from the child's song *Das himmlische Leben*. Here it is included in the setting of another

Wunderhorn poem that is introduced by the 'morning-bell' ostinato of children's voices, whose 'Bimm, bamm, bimm, bamm' rings out in F major after the last sepulchral A of the Nietzsche setting has died away:

Es sungen drei Engel einen süssen Gesang;	Three angels were singing a sweet song,
Mit Freuden es selig in dem Himmel klang,	In blissful joy it rang through heaven,
Sie jauchzten fröhlich auch dabei,	They shouted too for joy,
Dass Petrus sei von Sünden frei.	That Peter was set free from sin.
Und als der Herr Jesus zu Tische sass,	And as the Lord Jesus sat at table,
Mit seinen zwölf Jüngern das Abendmahl ass,	And ate the supper with his disciples,
Da sprach der Herr Jesus: Was stehst du denn hier?	Lord Jesus said: Why do you stand here?
Wenn ich dich anseh', so weinest du mir!	When I look at you, you weep at me.
„Und sollt' ich nicht weinen, du gütiger Gott?	'And should I not weep, thou bounteous God?
Ich hab übertreten die zehn Gebot,	I have broken the Ten Commandments,
Ich gehe und weine ja bitterlich.	I wander weeping bitterly.
Ach komm' und erbarme dich über mich!"	Oh come and have mercy on me!'
Hast du denn übertreten die zehn Gebot,	If you have broken the Ten Commandments
So fall auf die Knie und bete zu Gott!	Then fall on your knees and pray to God.
Liebe nur Gott in alle Zeit!	Only love God all the time!
So wirst du erlangen die himmlische Freud'.	Thus will you gain heavenly joy.
Die himmlische Freud' ist ein' selige Stadt,	Heavenly Joy is a blessed city,
Die himmlische Freud', die kein Ende mehr hat!	Heavenly joy, that has no end!
Die himmlische Freude war Petro bereit't	Heavenly Joy was granted to Peter,
Durch Jesum, und Allen zur Seligkeit.	Through Jesus, and to all men for eternal bliss .[41]

No one but Mahler would have dared to try a movement like this – drawing a full women's chorus and a company of rowdy children into his symphony for a movement that he himself reckoned to last only four minutes. Its manner and role are without compare, its 'humour' essential to the subversively democratic Nietzscheanism of the whole conception. The sheer cheek of the childlike angels may have more to do with Germanic Christmas-carols than Mediterranean dances, but they would soon wreck any production of *Parsifal* (they might find a place in *Die Meistersinger*). The elaborate artifice of the previous movement's song of individuated inwardness is now replaced by a public celebration – a musical party to which everyone has been invited, from the local church choir to the village band. They tell the penitent woman that all will be well if she loves God and kneels in prayer (were her words intended in the poem to be St Peter's?). Private agony may here be overcome in the religious practice of the social group.

But the very fact that this is a *Wunderhorn* poem, a naive song of bells and angels, reminds us that we are back in the 'dream', on our ascending path through the levels of internalized being. We are only passing through this humorously posited mode of experience: a miniature reminder of the unruly forces of Nature that had rampaged in the first movement. What focuses them now is the social form of the strophic song. This in itself contains, in a clearly delineated middle section, the penitent supplication of the contralto who insists upon the sorrowing key of D minor (of the previous movement) in a song that otherwise rejoices mainly in F major (the originally intended 'key' of the symphony).[42] Along with the children, the bells and the merrily dotted march-tune, the angels speak for a matter-of-fact world of sprightliness and guttersnipe effrontery (the directions *keck* and *munter* are explicit). Mahler offers this as one possibility of redemption, recalling Nietzsche's laughing children and angels who had dispelled Zarathustra's gloom. The distilled essence of the Beethovenian choral finale is presented as a cheerful communal song to which anyone might contribute – like the sopranos in bar 27, whose 'Why are you standing here?' in C major saucily disregards their sister angels' more decorous preparation for the words of Jesus in a chorale-like D major.

The extended quotation from *Das himmlische Leben* reminds us that the penitent woman has, indeed, a great deal to be sorry about. Or should we say a great deal that she, as a representative of mankind, can as yet not condone in herself or comprehend without the 'humour' of the angels? The two stanzas (musically speaking) in which she explains her 'bitter tears' are in fact successive reworkings of the section that occurs in *Das himmlische Leben* between cues 6 and 7 (bars 66 to 75) in the Fourth Symphony. What in the Third becomes a beautiful homophonic gesture of supplication (bar 58), follows some of the fateful spinning semiquavers of *Das himmlische Leben*, already encountered in the 'flowers' minuet. In the Fourth Symphony they include the stylized bellowing of oxen being butchered by St Luke for the heavenly banquet. As if in awareness of their fate, the Third's bell music subsequently 'swells steadily' and menacingly into a fearsome climax, from two before cue 6, until it is dispelled by the reassuring voices of the angels and children. By bar 90 they are back in F major as they march away into the distance of past dreams.

Appropriately, it is a beatified version of the alto's gesture of supplication ('Ach komm und erbarme dich!') that serenely breaks the silence in the incomparable beginning of the final Adagio. The manuscript bears the following epigraph, adapted from *Des Knaben Wunderhorn* (see Plate 3):

Vater, sieh an die Wunden mein!	Father, look upon my wounds,
Kein Wesen lass verloren sein!	Let no creature be lost![43]

The movement contrives to bring together *Parsifal* (via Bruckner), heroic Nietzscheanism and Romantic socialism, yet as absolute music (always admired, even by conservative critics)[44] it also accommodates established musical-aesthetic convention. Like all 'good' expressive music, its celebration of transcendent reconciliation seems to endanger no status quo, however Christian or Nietzschean the composer's conception might have been. Mahler's fair copy of the movement (dated Hamburg, Sunday 22 November 1896) even deliberately underlines the first part of the direction on the score's closing page: "Not with crude [roh] force! Richly full, noble tone! [Gesättigten, edlen Ton!]'.

In striking contrast to Mahler's two previous finales, this movement does not present a clearly evolving programmatic narrative. The form alludes to that of variations, but of a kind in which the developmental experiments of late Beethoven are audibly influential. There is certainly a complementary element that can threaten the stability of the chorale-like opening theme, while also imploring its benediction: setting up a dialogue between the divine and the human, the *Übermensch* and the *Mensch*. This element is perhaps implicit within the main theme itself, which is presented as an idealization of human, *singing* euphony. The initial directions are 'Slow. Peaceful. *Felt*

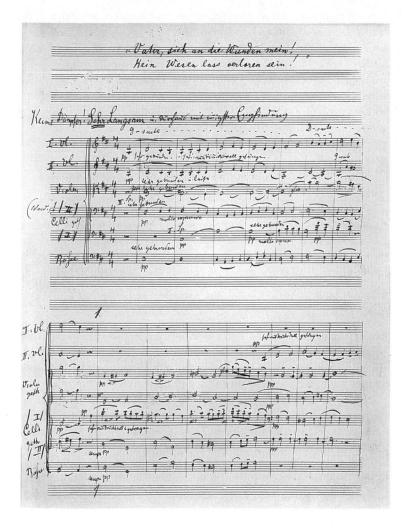

Plate 3 The opening of the final movement of the Third Symphony in Mahler's fair-copy manuscript, dated 22 November 1896. (Reproduced by permission; from Gustav Mahler SYMPHONY NO 3 in the Robert Owen Lehman Collection on deposit in the Pierpont Morgan Library, New York.)

[Empfunden]' (my emphasis), the chorale 'very expressively sung [*sehr aus-drucksvoll gesungen*]'. Paul Bekker was to point out that the theme is eternal in its potential for limitless unfolding, while also constantly tending towards resolving cadences.[45] Appropriately, its very first notes are dominant-to-tonic: the perfect fourth that would initiate the whole process of creation at the beginning of the first movement.

The opening eight-bar phrase is followed at once by the counter-theme. Also marked 'very expressive', it acts as if it were a consequent to the first theme, but is really an alternative antecedent: a sequentially 'aspiring' melody whose ever more animated search for what the opening idea already promises will occasion the three nodal crises in which the movement's stability and outcome appear to be thrown into doubt. Even in its first statement at cue 1, this theme is attended by poignant chromatic passing-notes, the violas' G sharp in bar 10 presaging pain to come (Ex. 8).

Twelve bars later the seraphic chorale returns, as ever it must. The movement's victory over conflictual 'development' will indeed be signalled by increasingly intense experiences of this theme's ability to return and bless us after no matter what torments. At first, the progress of the movement as vari-ations, or even 'divisions on a ground', realizes the initial ternary structure (reconciliation – passionate supplication – reconciliation) on a larger scale. Following the more neutral, Brucknerian interlude of cues 4-5, whose new, four-bar motif will shortly be drawn into the musical argument, the first 'variation', from cue 5, at once sets out 'more animatedly' in search of affirmation (although a version of the chorale acts as a stabilizing bass-line from the start). The first significant collapse into crisis, nominally in F sharp minor, occurs around cue 7, after which a new horn motif, marked *Leidenschaftlich* ('passionate') dominates a passage of tense, tremolando neg-ativity. The nature and origin of this motif I will return to. Significant at this point is the deliberate 'recovery' enacted with the return of the *gesangvoll* sec-ond theme at cue 9, following a long-held F natural, in, or on the way towards, the home key of D major. It is a pattern that will be repeated, and nowhere more strikingly than at cue 19. In the middle of embattled quasi-development, the fervent lyricism of the second theme, recalling the finale of the First symphony, prepares a cliff-hanging upbeat into a grand return of the chorale melody on eight horns. The key, however, is an alien E flat major and the second great crisis looms, in which the horns revert to a portentous three-note motif that echoes from the depths of the first-movement's intro-duction (see horns there, eight before cue 5 and at cue 29). It is also a direct quotation of the contralto's phrase 'Tief ist ihr Weh' from the Nietzsche set-

Example 8

ting (bar 105, five after cue 8), here insisting on G minor although the indicated key is D (Ex. 9).

This 'woe' the transfigured spirit must learn to encompass, although it is
shortly crushed rather than encouraged by what was to become a gesture of
culminatory assent in the first movement: a descending, fanfare-like figure in

the trumpets. Mahler quotes it almost verbatim from the movement which the entire Adagio must be regarded as modelled upon. This is the slow movement of the symphony by his long-deceased student friend Hans Rott.[46] The re-modelling even involved adapting the shape of Rott's opening theme for the chorale-melody (Ex. 10); it also entailed borrowing the texture and placing of the transfigured, high solo trumpet return at cue 26. The motivation for this is a tantalizing, perhaps unsolvable mystery, which I will return to when discussing the first movement. The key descending figure in Mahler's Adagio seems to presage irrevocable collapse, while now revealing the origin of the horn motif of the first crisis (see bars 75ff) with which it is here coupled, and which had also appeared in the Rott movement (Ex. 11). The music sinks into despair, three times grinding out an archetypal descending sigh (G to F sharp) that also plays a part in the first movement (see cue 30ff). But then, over quivering violas (A–C natural, tremolando), a tremulous flute announces a version of the second main theme which initi-

Example 9

Example 10

ates, along with mysterious E–A pizzicati in the cellos and basses, the movement's final paragraph. Both themes are here presented in radiantly assenting
form, rising inexorably via the emphatically, almost raucously stressed vocal
turn of the second theme, towards the monumental grandeur of the closing
bars.

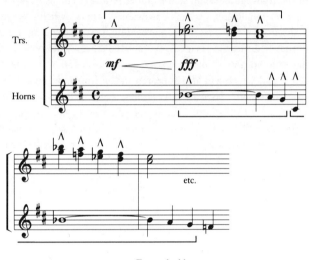

Example 11

One wonders what this ending was like before Mahler revised it, after
completing the first movement, on 31 July 1896. Now, he told Natalie Bauer-
Lechner, it culminated 'in broad chords and only in the one tonality of D
major [!]'.[47] In the movement as we know it, the chorale theme is refined to
a descending scale on the trombones before its opening phrase returns above
a vast subdominant 6-4 chord to conduct us into the culminatory plagal
cadence. With timpani and bass instruments striding from tonic to dominant,
it marches towards the last, prolonged chord of D major, radiant not simply
in its own nobility, but with the eternal love which, as Mahler put it, 'acts
within us - as the rays come together in a focal point'.[48] Such music inspires
rather than expresses reverential awe. By thus becoming God, Mahler
redefines the deity as Nietzschean *Übermensch*: as the highest mode of human
awareness; a climax rather than a transcendence of conscious Being.

Part One: Movement 1. *Kräftig. Entschieden.*
Introduction: Pan awakes, leading directly into No.1: Summer marches in ('Bacchic procession').

It has almost ceased to be music; it is hardly anything but sounds of Nature. It's eerie, the way life gradually breaks through, out of soulless, petrified matter. (I might equally well have called the movement 'What the mountain rocks tell me.') And, as this life rises from stage to stage, it takes on ever more highly developed forms: flowers, beasts, man, up to the sphere of the spirits, the 'angels'. Once again, an atmosphere of brooding summer midday heat hangs over the introduction to this movement; not a breath stirs, all life is suspended, and the sun-drenched air trembles and vibrates. I hear it in my inner ear, but how to find the right notes for it? At intervals there come the moans of the youth, of captive life struggling for release from the clutches of lifeless, rigid Nature (as in Hölderlin's 'Rhine'). In the first movement, which follows the introduction, *attacca*, it finally breaks through and triumphs!

Mahler to Natalie Bauer-Lechner, June 1896[49]

Exuberance and optimism inform all of Mahler's many descriptions of the first movement of the Third during the period of its composition in 1896. Whether recorded in letters or reported by friends like Natalie Bauer-Lechner, Bruno Walter and Josef Foerster, these accounts add up to one of the most extraordinary documentations of post-Romantic musical 'inspiration' as an experience of mystical epiphany. What seemed to manifest itself to Mahler was nothing less than a musical vision of Nature — but now significantly interpreted as a dynamic process of becoming; of a progression from captivity to freedom, like that of the personified river Rhine in Hölderlin's great poem (also quoted by Mahler to Natalie in the summer of 1893):[50] its cries for release from within the 'cold chasm' of the mountains are heard by the poet, who sits on a high prominence, at the forest's edge, enjoying the 'golden noon' as his mind begins to turn towards southern climes.[51] Repeatedly, Mahler's manner of expression recalls the visionary enthusiasm of the early letter to Joseph Steiner (see above, p. 13), now expressed in language which constantly echoes the Nietzsche of *Zarathustra, Die fröhliche Wissenschaft* and *Die Geburt der Tragödie*. His comments also indicate that this movement, for whose composition he claimed he needed the courage that only the completion of all the others had given him,[52] soon came to represent a kind of synopsis of everything the symphony was to express. On returning to Hamburg after finishing it he described the whole work in terms that might equally have applied to the first movement alone: 'Victorious appearance of Helios; the miracle of spring is accomplished. And then, as everything already lives, breathes, blossoms and sings, pressing towards maturity, there come those who shared in the miracle — the imperfect ones — human beings.'[53]

The myth of stratified eternal being is replaced with a vision of the reality, or possibility, of dynamic becoming: of that revolutionary transformation of 'the way things are' which will burst apart the conflict and resolution principle of sonata in a movement that begins in D minor and ends in F major. The retention of 'Symphony in F major' on the manuscript's title-page[54] may have been an oversight (compare the Fifth Symphony 'in C sharp minor' – the key of the first movement, not its finale). It nevertheless points tantalizingly towards my suggested interpretation of the movement as one which not only engages in that formal self-destruction or self-transcendence which he had deliberately checked in all the other movements, but also threatens to transcend the containing symphony. We recall that he regarded the Third as comprehensively replacing the Second, whose own transcendental Finale provides the clearest model for this preliminary march-past of all life. Given that it was the movement of the Third for which Mahler rightly anticipated the greatest critical condemnation (in 1960 even Deryck Cooke regarded it as a 'total failure'),[55] we can understand why he at times claimed to become horrified by the music, in which 'everything human shrinks into a pygmy-world'.[56] It was in respect of *this* movement, rather than the final Adagio, that Mahler saw himself in the role of martyr to his own creation:

> ... Christ on the Mount of Olives, compelled to drain the cup of sorrow to the dregs – and willing it to be so. No one for whom this cup is destined can or will refuse it, but at times a deathly fear must overcome him when he thinks of what is before him. I have the same feeling when I think of this movement, in anticipation of what I shall have to suffer because of it, without even living to see it recognized and appreciated for what it is.[57]

Only two days before this conversation with Natalie (4 July), he had written in somewhat lighter mood to the young Bruno Walter, inviting him to come and join him at Steinbach. That he was still envisaging what the new work would itself have to suffer (at the hands of the 'gentlemen of the press' at least) is clear from the parody review with which the letter had concluded:

> The entire thing is unfortunately again tainted with my disreputable sense of humour 'and there are plenty of opportunities for indulging my fancy for a fearful racket' .... That I cannot do without some triviality is sufficiently well

known. In this instance, to be sure, it passes all permissible bounds. 'One feels, at times, as if one were in a pub or a stable.'[58]

Later in 1896, after playing the completed movement to Natalie, he would invoke the image of Jacob 'wrestling with God until He blesses him' – adding significantly: 'If the Jews had been responsible for nothing but this image, they would still inevitably have grown to be a formidable people – God similarly withholds His blessing from me. I can only extort it from Him in my terrible struggles to bring my works into being.'[59]

In the conversation of 4 July already referred to, however, Mahler had made it clear that the first movement of the Third provided an answer to the questions of the previous symphony on a scale that made the Second seem 'like a child' beside it. In his effort to describe it in more explicit detail, Mahler had first invited Natalie to join him in a Schopenhauerian belief in the revelatory power of music[60]. Natalie had interrupted with the excited comment that it must be 'terrifying ... like the Earth Spirit appearing before Faust'. Mahler's striking response, quoted in Chapter 3 (p. 51), had begun: 'Not only the Earth Spirit, but the Universe itself, into whose infinite depths you sink, through whose eternal spaces you soar, so that earth and human destiny shrink behind you into an indiscernibly tiny point and then disappear.'[61]

Mahler's 'struggle with God' was, as we have seen, also a process of *becoming* God; after the first rehearsal play-through of the first movement in 1902, he was to call up humorously to his wife: 'And he saw that it was good!'[62] But 'humour' was indeed the key to all his public attempts to explain this most complex and ambitious of his symphonic movements, whose 'humorous, even grotesque [*baroque*]'[63] programme was to be interpreted in the light of Nietzsche's understanding of the Apollonian aspect of Greek drama in *The Birth of Tragedy*. Perhaps it was to accommodate the extent to which the musical imagery itself came to reflect and participate in the humorous dream-conception, signalled in the titles and manuscript annotations, that Mahler abandoned the formula 'Zug des Dionysos' ('Procession of Dionysus') that had appeared as a possible alternative to the first movement's 'Der Sommer marschiert ein' in a letter of 2 September 1895, to Natalie Bauer-Lechner.[64] It is surely more in keeping with its yea-saying, Nietzschean qualities of southern lightness and gaiety that Mahler should have stressed to Natalie in 1896 that the march itself was 'not in dionysian mood ... on the contrary, satyrs and other such rough children of Nature disport themselves in it'.[65]

It properly matched the intended mood of Nietzschean *Heiterkeit*[66] that this summer-march, heir to the egalitarian judgement-march of the Second, should become a *Bacchic* procession. Its merrily intoxicated participants were to stride into battle under the banner of Pan, the lazy and goat-like old fertility god whose 'simplicity and love of riot' were despised by the Olympian gods who nevertheless exploited his powers.[67] In July 1896 Mahler told the singer Anna von Mildenburg, with whom he was having an affair in Hamburg and corresponding regularly, that the whole symphony would be called ' "Pan" ... an ancient Greek god, as you will surely know, who later came to stand for the All (Pan, Greek all.)'[68] By 4 July he had even come to think of calling the whole work *Pan, Symphonic Poems.*[69] And while Nietzsche and *The Birth of Tragedy* may have represented the primary inspiration for Mahler's recollection of his *Gymnasium* and university classics courses, others were also busy reinvoking the old gods at that time, particularly in the visual arts. Centaurs had long been appearing in the popular paintings of Böcklin, while the Dutch Alma-Tadema, an indefatigable celebrator of the ancient world, had on more than one occasion painted Bacchic subject-matter (e.g. *Eine Weihung an Bacchus* of 1889, now in Hamburg). During precisely the period when Mahler was composing the Third, Max Klinger, subsequently fêted by the Vienna Secession, was working on his monumental *Gesamtkunstwerk*: the painting *Christ in Olympus* (1893-6), depicting the direct confrontation of Christianity and the world of the ancient pagan gods (it was exhibited at the Secession in Vienna in 1899).[70]

The relation of Pan and the Bacchic mood to the final conception of the Third's first movement is of central relevance not only to its 'humour' but also to the deliberately rough and 'natural' quality of much of its musical material – to whose banality and apparent triviality the critics responded pretty much as Mahler had expected. But as the anonymous Zürich critic had heard here a deliberate music of 'the people',[71] so Richard Strauss admitted to Specht that as he conducted the first movement of the Third, there had come into his mind a vision of workers marching to the Prater on May-Day – an image that Specht felt would have delighted Mahler, whether or not he had intended the music that way.[72]

There is clear evidence that Mahler strove for an earthy, plebeian quality in the marches' melodic material and scoring:

'Summer draws in will be the prelude. Straight away I need a regimental band to give the rough and crude effect of my martial company's arrival [*der Auskunft meines martialen Gesellen*]. It will be just like the military band on parade. Such a mob is milling around, you never saw anything like it!

Naturally, it doesn't come off without a struggle with the opposition, Winter; but he is easily dispatched, and Summer, in his strength and superior power, soon gains undisputed mastery.[73]

Perhaps the most intriguing single piece of the evidence relates to the very opening theme for the eight horns, headed *Der Weckruf!* in the manuscript.[74] Numerous contemporary critics and subsequent Austrian and German commentators were to be struck by the 'popular' character of this theme, even hearing it, like Ernst Křenek, as 'literally identical with the first phrase of a marching song which all Austrian school children used to sing'.[75] Once again we are indebted to William J. McGrath for elucidation, not in his original book, however, but in a fascinating article (1979) examining the historical determinants and context of certain parallels in the careers and backgrounds of Mahler and Sigmund Freud.[76.]

It is not necessary here to go into Freud's dream which, on the advice of Fliess he removed from those recorded and examined in *The Interpretation of Dreams* (published in 1900). What is important is that the self-censorship seems likely to have been on political grounds relevant to Freud's loss of hope, in the late 1890s, for democratic government in Austria-Hungary. His pessimism was deeply rooted in memories of his student membership of the German-nationalist *Leseverein der deutschen Studenten Wiens,* whose relevance to Mahler's early student experience in Vienna we have already considered. Still more interesting, however, is the fact that Freud referred, in the dream and later, to the title of the very song that de La Grange named as one of the possible audible sources for the Third's opening theme: *Wir hatten gebauet ein stattliches Haus.*[77] It is still remembered in Germany and Austria, sometimes with Massmann's words *Ich hab' mich ergeben ... [dir] mein deutsches Vaterland.* It was, however, with August Binzer's text, 'We had built a stately house', that the song had been sung by defiant students on 20 December 1878, following the government's decision to dissolve the *Leseverein* on grounds of its danger to the state.[78]

There is no evidence that Mahler, who left the University in the autumn of 1878, was still in Vienna at that time, but the generally accepted political colouration of the Binzer version of the song is fascinating, not least since it was originally written in deliberate defiance of Metternich's suppression of the democratic and German-nationalist student fraternities in 1819, following the murder of Kotzebue. Here are the first two stanzas (of eight), in McGrath's translation, of the song that Binzer, a student himself, had written at that time:

> We had built a stately house and in it put our trust
> in God through tempest, storm and dread.
>
> We lived so true, so united, so free; to the
> wicked it was terrible that we were so true.[79]

The full melody of the song as it appears in one of Ludwig Erk's
Volkslieder-Album collections (where it is explicitly described as having been
'sung at Jena at the dissolution of the fraternities [Burschenschaften] on 26
November 1819') is given in Ex. 12.[80]

It becomes clear why the connection of the song as quoted by Brahms in
his *Academic Festival Overture* with the main theme of Mahler's first movement has not been more generally noticed. Brahms uses the whole melody,
but alters the first and third bars, where he repeats the G and the B flat
respectively, rather than allowing the return to the first note of the bar.
Mahler retains the original version, alluding only to these first two bars of
the song, though – present (in B flat) on the first '1893' sketch for the movement.[81] The point not made by McGrath, however, is that the exact form of
this opening (interestingly presented *in F major* by Erk) is found not in the
opening bars of the movement, however clearly the horns' dorian theme may
allude to it, but at what Mahler seems to have regarded as the beginning of
the first movement proper (cue 23), where the march tune now rings out

Example 12

brightly, in F major and beginning exactly as indicated above (horns in F from one before cue 23). Other songs might also be cited as possible 'sources' – interestingly, the best other candidate in Erk's collection is a song of soldierly comradeship in battle, called *Der gute Kamerad*,[82] opening as in Ex. 13. Nevertheless, the Binzer connection, which must surely have been the one that struck many of the early listeners to the symphony, can hardly have escaped the attention of so canny a musician as Mahler, and helps us to ground and justify the picture that came into Strauss's mind while conducting the movement. Could this also help explain the significant allusions to the symphony of Mahler's own former 'guter kamerad' Hans Rott, whose slow movement is so significantly echoed in the Third's concluding Adagio (see p. 75)? The most explicit link between the first movement and the Adagio is indeed the Rott motif quoted earlier in Ex. 11. Only in the first movement, however, does the specifically social character and potential power of Mahler's forces of Nature become fully clear, as he dispenses with the manners of 'good' bourgeois music and once more throws the doors of the concert-hall open to village bands and those rough 'children of Nature', whose purpose, coming from afar, is to rout the repressive Philistines (as the forces of winter inertia) once and for all.

Example 13

This is certainly one of the most remarkable and lengthy of all nineteenth-century symphonic movements: a dramatized and programmaticized kind of sonata structure, scored for an enormous orchestra[83], that might have given any Brahmsian the shivers. It has been denounced as disorganized and un-unified by any number of commentators less worthy than Deryck Cooke (who still regarded it a 'partial failure' in the final 1980 version of his Mahler study).[84] Most responsive and imaginative of the analytical commentators, however, is David B. Greene, whose phenomenological study of the movement's intentional caesuras and deliberate play of confusing and contradictory kinds of temporality (at Wrst refusing to progress towards any organically generated or 'logical' future) is to be recommended as one of the most challenging and imaginative accounts of it.85

I have suggested where the consistently indicated (but never specified) division of the first movement into 'Introduction' ('Pan sleeps') and 'first movement' ('Summer marches in') might be made. It is certainly from around cue 23 that the marching forces of summer begin, as Greene would put it, to generate at last a purposefully goal-directed musical continuity. The relationship between the implied division of this movement and the actual division of the 'first part' of the Fifth Symphony further leads me to suggest that the whole introduction was for Mahler nothing less than a giant developmentally repeated exposition, with its own prelude (up to cue 2). First there is the *Weckruf*[86] – presenting the outline of the Binzer theme in the manner of an epic *Naturlaut* whose energizing power (how the accompanying brass, wind and strings crack to attention in bars 6–8!) fades into a mysterious and sepulchral stillness. The opening *O Mensch* chords and succeeding harmonized oscillation from the Nietzsche setting are then heard, accompanied by tam-tam, timpani and the great bass drum. The latter alone crosses the ensuing chasm of silence to support the imperious funeral-march (*Schwer und dumpf* – 'heavy and oppressive') whose reiterated, orchestrated drum-beats (♫ ♩ ♪ ♫ ♩ ♪) provide the framework for the panorama of Chaos. This forms the first-subject group before the completely contrasted material of cue 11, which follows after another almost total silence and is headed 'Pan sleeps' in the manuscript. It supplies a contrasted second-subject complex the likes of which no Romantic programmaticist had hitherto dared conceive of. For this is no symmetrical contrast between 'masculine' and 'feminine' elements but a total opposition between the chaotic frustration and the fruitful generation of musical Life.

Perhaps, nearly a century later, we are better able to deal with this extraordinary symphonic exposition because the juxtaposition of initially mysterious fragments of unconnected narratives, first tried in the equivalent introductory business of the Second Symphony's finale, has become a standard device of film-producers. As in some Hollywood epic, Mahler first gives us a slowly panning shot of the primaeval landscape in which eruptive gestures and uprooted rhetorical figures constantly and fruitlessly expend their energy – like the arpeggiated trumpet-motif rising to the sharpened leading-note whose resolution is a 'dying' afterthought. ('Think of the Tritons blowing on conch shells in the Classical Walpurgisnacht',[87] Mahler is reported to have told Willibald Kaehler in 1904, alluding to the second part of Goethe's *Faust*). Even the craggy horn theme that gathers itself into an extended statement at cue 5 is marked *Rubato* and has the character of a recitative-like figuration whose business is the decoration of an extended cadence. Six bars after cue 9, however, Mahler permits the scene to be engulfed in vapour of the kind employed by Wagner in the scene-changes in *Das Rheingold* and, as it were, to grow suddenly distant (although his first attempt at the passage between cues 9 and 10 had proved *too* abrupt and he was to extend it by adding the long chromatic scale leading from the ff B flat of the bass-clarinet and bassoons).[88] The mist seems to clear and a new picture to focus at cue 11, but now as if in another world – perhaps the summer-noonday hillside on which old Pan sleeps (do the flutes and piccolos depict his breathing?). He dreams a melody that grows out of a decorated form of the 'breathing' motif (D flat to C, then E flat to D – see Ex. 14). The rhythm of this motif is taken over by the *espressivo* solo violin. It spins out the 'second subject' proper in D major, with key-signature to match, while the accompanying instruments sleep on in a key-signature of one flat. The theme itself settles down after seven bars into what might be an ostinato figuration, but this is broken into at cue 12 by a sprightly little repeated wind signal in D flat major, marked in the manuscript *Der Herold!* This invokes a flowing semiquaver pattern in the cellos and basses which itself then dies away into four bars of solo military percussion that seem distantly to be preparing the tempo of a march.

A complete ('Long!') blackout-pause ensues before we are faced once more with the vision of Chaos, back in a funereal D minor. A shortened, developing 'repeat' of the whole strange complex follows – the 'bell-up' solo

Example 14

trombone's notes three after cue 13, bearing the inscription 'Stimme des Todes ruft Predigt' ('Proclamation by the Voice of Death') in Mengelberg's score (in his hand). This time, the 'Pan sleeps' material[89] is still more delicately borne upon airy trills and flutterings. Now the herald's signal calls up a swirl of semiquavers out of which 'clearly', and yet 'as if from the far distance', a real march begins to materialize, accompanied by signalling birdcalls like those in the third movement. Here they mimic the first motif of the march (Ex. 15). Beneath it, the characteristic dotted rhythm of the Second Symphony's funeral march is transformed into a light-hearted skipping (Ex. 16).

Example 15

We are now set firmly on course for the return of the opening *Weckruf* in its F major, 'Binzer' version, to initiate the first movement proper and the first of the great marches in which it accompanies the transformed 'second subject', decorated in merry communal improvisation as it tumbles towards the eruptive climax, twelve bars after cue 28. This is marked by the Hans Rott gesture (Ex. 11) which will dominate the final crisis in the concluding Adagio. It now has a thoroughly positive affective significance, apparently aspiring to convince us of conclusive accomplishment rather than fatal denial. The march in D major catches its breath and then explodes in a tutti chord of B flat major (6-3), the rising octave leap (F natural) in the trumpets being a standard *topos* of triumphant affirmation. In a sudden, dramatic reversal, however, it is broken in upon by the primaeval horns of the first-subject group (see nine after cue 4), into whose fearsome realm we are now hurled once more.

The most striking feature of this partial restatement of the Chaos material is the long trombone solo with which it concludes. Marked *Sentimental*, it

Example 16

is notated as one of Mahler's 'singing' arioso lines, with written-out rubato and sighing appoggiaturas. It is as if the 'Voice of Death' here laments its own nature. There follows, via a mysteriously *unbroken* transformation at this point, the most magical and translucent of all the versions of the 'Pan sleeps' material (cue 35) – now most deliberately in Mahler's 'dream' mode.[90] It conjures, at cue 39, a G flat major vision of the triumphal final state of the second-subject-as-march, the form in which we had last heard it in D major at cue 28. But the bass octave B flats after cue 42 dispel the dream and initiate a second march complex.

This opens with an energetically extended version of the very first march motif, for double-basses and cellos alone until they are joined at cue 44 by 'the rabble' (the manuscript bears the heading *Das Gesindel!*). For Nietzsche in *Zarathustra*, the 'rabble' were lascivious poisoners of wells[91] – a crime historically imputed to Vienna's unwanted Jews[92] – who seem to represent the basest aspects of humanity from which he would distance himself. We may feel that Mahler has more magnanimously invited them to join his Bacchic battalion. They certainly include most of the ironically grimacing and sneering creatures that had made up the cortège of the Huntsman's Funeral in the First Symphony.[93] For a spell, Mahler pulls out all the stops of musical nastiness in the sliding and slithering trills of the woodwind's mocking dance. But as the new motley procession gets under way, its gloriously plebeian oom-pahs on the contra-bassoon (e.g. seven after cue 46) and general goodheartedness endear these newcomers to us. At cue 48 the *Weckruf* theme makes a return appearance and the troops fall into place for the 'battle' at cue 49 (headed *Die Schlacht beginnt!*). The humorous picture grows programmatically explicit. Excited signals resound from amongst waving pennants on all sides. Led by the *Weckruf* and the *Herold* motif, the troops pitch headlong into the fray at cue 51, where Mahler's manuscript bears the heading *Der*

Südsturm! ('The southern storm') – as if intent on stressing that his warriors were also representatives of Nature all the time. He described the passage on 4 July 1896:

> It all tumbles forward madly in the first movement, like the southern storm that has been sweeping over us here recently. (Such a wind, I'm sure, is the source of all fertility, blowing as it does from the far-off warm and abundant lands – not like those easterlies courted by us folk!) It rushes upon us in a march tempo that carries all before it; nearer and nearer, louder and louder, swelling like an avalanche, until you are overwhelmed by the great roaring and rejoicing of it all. Meanwhile, there come mystical presentiments – *O Mensch, gib Acht* (from the 'Night') – as infinitely strange, mysterious interludes of repose.[94]

The 'meanwhile' is tantalizing, for what Mahler does not fully explain is why the whole passage, at whose outset the strings were directed to play 'with terrible force', rushes first not into the 'roaring and rejoicing' that undoubtedly comes later, but out of sight altogether until, at cue 54, we hear 'A few side-drums in the distance' which beat out 'the old march tempo' and lead into the most unexpected recapitulation there ever was.[95] Back we go to the very opening *Weckruf* and the *O Mensch* chords, before sinking once more into the Chaos material. In part it is, of course, a deliberately self-defeating act: the formal gesture of return made only to be all the more explicitly worsted by the freeing and transforming march that is the movement's real business. But so too might we see this (chronologically) as the symphony's final gesture towards Tradition. On 27 July Mahler observed to Natalie:

> without my having planned it, this movement – just like the whole work – has the same scaffolding, the same basic groundplan that you'll find in the works of Mozart and, on a grander scale, of Beethoven. Old Haydn was really its origi-nator. Its laws must indeed be profound and eternal; for Beethoven obeyed them, and they're confirmed once more in my own work. Adagio, Rondo, Minuet, Allegro – and within these forms the traditional plan, the familiar phrase-structure. The only difference is that, in my works, the sequence of movements is not the same, and the variety and complexity within the movements is greater.[96]

Analysts have long wondered whether the developing variety and complexity within *this* movement does not demand some quite new formal interpretation. In fact the new form depends upon an elaborate reinterpretation of the old, which Mahler is still prepared to see here as an almost mystical 'given'. But the desire for transformation is once again symbolized at this very point by the lamenting solo trombone of cue 33 which re-emerges from the gloom, only no longer marked *Sentimental*. Has it, in Schiller's sense, become 'naive': a part of Nature rather than self-consciously longing for it? It nevertheless concludes with a vocal 'turn' that generates what must be a deliberate quotation, in the cellos, of the oboe phrase from the *Urlicht* of the Second Symphony which comes there after the words 'je lieber möcht ich im Himmel sein!' ('I would rather be in Heaven!'), four bars before cue 3 (Ex. 17).

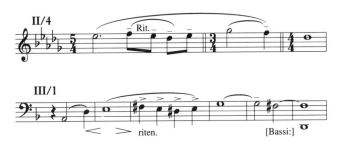

Example 17

The song that will find its apotheosis at the other end of the symphony sinks back into the silence. The Bacchic march of summer tentatively reforms and approaches 'from the farthest distance'. Pan's second subject, now in F major and in its march guise, returns at cue 64 to take full and jubilant possession of the territory that the forces of winter have renounced at last. As in the first march complex, the goal is the great gesture of assent that Mahler had borrowed from Hans Rott. Here it leads, via a Neapolitan chord of G flat major (changing to G major, instead of the expected dominant), into a helter-skelter rush to the last F major cadence. Before composing the final sixteen bars, Mahler had joked with Natalie on 27 July: 'Just so long as nothing happens to me today ... for no one but me could complete the sixteen bars of the gigantic fanfare which I get Pan, in my Bacchic march, to extract from the whole uproarious rabble!'[97] With that fanfare, the Mahler who would himself one day march with the workers on the Ringstrasse,[98] celebrated his world-transforming 'composing away' of Nature (as he had joked to Bruno

Walter).[99] Had Hirschfeld listened more carefully, he might have come to hear in it not only a destructive picture of the world as it was, but also a liberating vision of what it *might be*. Its optimism was signalled in challenging Nietzschean fashion at the end of the first movement's manuscript, dated Hamburg, 17 October 1896:

> To him who will get there!
> To those who will be there![100]

Appendix I

The 1896 manuscript and the first published score:
Unpublished or subsequently omitted directions and annotations

In the transcription that follows, the page-number is followed by the bar-number. Directions marked with § appear in the first published score. Programmatic movement titles and internal inscriptions, generally in bold longhand in the 1896 manuscript, are capitalized here to distinguish them from primarily performance-orientated directions.

The first edition of the symphony was published by Josef Weinberger in Vienna after the first performance in 1902 (plate '9'). There were two printings of this. The second, in smaller study-score format, included revisions like the change from Flügelhorn to 'Posthorn in B' in the third movement. The score was adopted by Universal and reprinted with revisions c. 1906 (UE 950, still plate '9'). The final Universal score published during Mahler's lifetime (UE 950) came out in 1910. The revised score published by Universal (UE 13822) for the International Gustav Mahler Society in 1974 bears their plate number UE 2939 (first appearing in 1937). It is to be noted that all these scores appear to derive from the same original plates, renumbered and amended, and therefore share the same page-numbers.

Appendix I

[Title-page:]

Symphonie Nro III in F-Dur / Einleitung: Pan erwacht / folgt sogleich /
Nro I: Der Sommer Marschirt ein / („Bachuszug") / Partitur

1. Kräftig. Entschieden.

[Bottom p. 1:]

§Anmerkung für den Dirigenten: Das Anfangstempo ist im Ganzen und
Grossen für das ganze Stück durchaus festzuhalten und trotzt den jeweili-
gen Taktwechseln oder Modificationen strengste Continuität desselben
durchzuführen.

[p. 1/bar 2:]   DER WECKRUF!
[15/132:]   PAN SCHLÄFT
[16/148:]   DER HEROLD!

[48/410; note at foot of page to asterisk against string parts at cue 32:]

§Anmerkung für den Dirigenten: Diese Stelle muss von den Streichern
mit höchster Kraftentfaltung gespielt werden, so dass die Saiten durch die
heftige Vibration beinahe in Berührung mit dem Griffbrett gerathen. Der
Wiener hat dafür den Ausdruck „schöppern". [Added in 1st edn score:]
Ein gleiches gilt von den Hörnern.

[59/539:]   DAS GESINDEL!
[68/538:]   DIE SCHLACHT BEGINNT!
[72/605:]   DER SÜDSTURM!
[73/608:]   §Vorwärts stürmen!
[104, end of MS:]

folgt eine lange Pause! / Hamburg, Sonnabend / 17 Oktober 1896
Dem, der da kommen wird!
Denen, die da sein werden!

Appendix I

[Title-page:]

Symphony No. III in F major / Introduction: Pan awakes / leading directly to / No. I: Summer marches in / ('Bacchic Procession') / Score

1. Strong, Decisive/resolute.

[Bottom p. 1:]

§Note for the conductor: The opening tempo is by and large to be maintained throughout the whole movement; the strictest continuity is to be ensured in spite of occasional modifications or alterations of the beat.

[p. 1/bar 2:]	THE AWAKENING CALL (REVEILLE)
[15/132:]	PAN SLEEPS
[16/148:]	THE HERALD

[48/410; note at foot of page to asterisk against string parts at cue 32:]

§Note for the conductor: This passage must be executed with the utmost exertion of strength by the players, so that the strings almost come into contact with the fingerboard through the powerful vibration. The Viennese have the expression "schöppern" for this (lit. to clatter or rattle). [Added in 1st edn score:] Something similar applies to the horns.

[59/539:]	THE MOB/RABBLE
[68/538:]	THE BATTLE BEGINS
[72/605:]	THE SOUTHERN STORM
[73/608:]	§Charge/storm forwards!
[104, end of MS:]	

A long pause follows! / Hamburg, Saturday / 17 October 1896
To him who will get there!
To those who will be there!

93

2. Tempo di Menuetto. Sehr mässig. Ja nicht eilen!

[Title page:]

Nro. 3 / Was mir die Blumen / [inserted above:] auf der Wiese / erzählen

[105, in 1st edn score, note relating to asterisks marking Oboe c¹ bar 4, to c² bar 6:]

§ [Von * bis * kann das engl. Horn zuhilfe genommen werden, wenn die Oboist die Stelle nicht zart genug hervorbringen kann.]

[133, end of MS:]

Hamburg 11 April 96 / (In doloribus / In dolores)

[As elsewhere in the manuscript, this movement includes occasional notes to Mahler's copyist beginning 'Lieber Weidig ...']

2. Tempo di Menuetto. Very steady / restrained. Do not hurry!

[Title page:]

No. 3 / What the flowers / [inserted above:] in the meadow / tell me

[105, in 1st edn score, note relating to asterisks marking Oboe c¹ bar 4, to c² bar 6:]

§ [From * to * the cor anglais can be used if the oboist cannot play the passage softly enough.]

[133, end of MS:]

Hamburg 11 April 96 / (In doloribus / In dolores)

[As elsewhere in the manuscript, this movement includes occasional notes to Mahler's copyist beginning 'Dear Weidig ...']

<u>3. Comodo. Scherzando. Ohne Hast.</u>

[Title-page:]

Nro 4. / Was mir die Thiere im Walde erzählen

[154/256:] DER POSTILLON!

['1 Tr in B' altered in MS to 'Flügelhorn' (§'Flügelhorn in B' in the first edn) for all passages later given to 'Posthorn in B'.]

[172/482:] DER POSTILLON!

[179, note in 1st edn to Viola/Cello 'col legno':]

<u>Anmerkung für den Dirigenten</u>: Kein Irrthum! Mit dem Rücken des Bogens gestrichen!

[180, end of MS:]

Hamburg / Sonnabend 25 April 1896

<u>4. Sehr langsam. Misterioso. Durchaus ppp.</u>

[Title-page:]

Nro 5 / Was mir der Mensch erzählt

[183/32:] DER VOGEL DER NACHT!
[187/71:] (DER VOGEL DER NACHT!)
[189/102:] DER VOGEL DER NACHT!
[191/132:] DER VOGEL DER NACHT!

3. Comodo, Scherzando. Unhurried.

[Title-page:]

No. 4 / What the animals in the forest tell me

[154/256:]   THE POSTILION!

['1 Tr in B' altered in MS to 'Flügelhorn' (§'Flügelhorn in B' in the first edn) for all passages later given to 'Posthorn in B'.]

[172/482:]   THE POSTILION!

[179, note in 1st edn to Viola/Cello 'col legno':]

Note for the conductor: Not a mistake! Play with the back of the bow!

[180, end of MS:]

Hamburg / Saturday 25 April 1896

4. Very slow. Misterioso. ppp throughout.

[Title-page:]

No. 5 / What man tells me

[183/32:]	THE BIRD OF NIGHT
[187/71:]	(THE BIRD OF NIGHT)
[189/102:]	THE BIRD OF NIGHT
[191/132:]	THE BIRD OF NIGHT

5. Lustig im Tempo und keck im Ausdruck.

[Title-page:]

Nro 6 / Was mir die Engel erzählen.

[196/28, above Frauenchor, 'Hohestimme' *not* struck out by correcting copyist in Mengelberg's score:]
§Grob

[209, end of MS:]

Hamburg 8 Mai 1896

6. Langsam. Ruhevoll. Empfunden.

[Title-page:]

Nro 6 / „Was mir die Liebe erzählt"

[210, first page of the movement headed:]
„Vater, sieh an die Wunden mein!
Kein Wesen lass verloren sein!"

[231, end of MS:]

Hamburg, Sonntag, 22 November 1896.

5. <u>Cheerful in tempo and cheeky/forthright in expression.</u>

[Title-page:]

No. 6 / What the angels tell me.

[196/28, above Frauenchor, 'Hohestimme' *not* struck out by correcting copyist in Mengelberg's score:]
§Coarse/crude

[209, end of MS:]

Hamburg 8 May 1896

6. <u>Slow. Peaceful. Felt.</u>

[Title-page:]

No. 6 / 'What love tells me'

[210, first page of the movement headed:]
'Father, look upon my wounds!
Let no creature be lost!'

[231, end of MS:]

Hamburg, Sunday, 22 November 1896.

Appendix II

Two early sketches for the Third Symphony

I have referred in the text to what may be the earliest extant sketch for the symphony; the relevant page is transcribed as Ex. 18. It is on the first side of a double sheet (four sides) of eighteen-stave manuscript paper and is enclosed in another double sheet (of twenty-four-stave manuscript paper) which bears the following inscription on the front:

Steinbach am Attersee

> On the 28th July 1896 the curious thing happened that I was able to give my
> dear friend Natalie the seed of a tree which nevertheless already blossoms and
> flourishes in the world fully grown, with all its branches, leaves and fruit.
>
> Gustav Mahler[1]

The sketch is headed (not apparently in Mahler's hand) '1893' and apart from this first, inked page, the other three bear material that is either unattributable to known completed works or related to the Second Symphony (particularly the Andante). The transcription given in Ex. 18 was first published in *Music and Letters* in October 1977.[2] This sketch, in Stanford University Library, California (Memorial Library of Music no. 630), is kept with the four separate leaves (seven notated sides) of twenty-four-stave manuscript paper bearing Third Symphony sketch material and dated '1895' (no.631). The consecutive numbering of the pages (1-11) from that bearing the above sketch indicates that they were all in Natalie Bauer-Lechner's possession and may have been given to her at the same time in 1896.[3]

The second particularly interesting sketch (first movement (1895?)) mentioned in the text is in the Österreichischer Nationalbibliothek in Vienna (Cod, 22794). It is discussed in detail by John Williamson in an article in *Music and Letters* (1980).[4] The transcription (Ex. 19) of the striking passage where Mahler moves from the 'Der Herold' motif into material from the latter part of *Das himmlische Leben* (see Fourth Symphony, mov 4, four bars after cue 12 in the first violins) was published with Ex. 18 in 1977.[5] Full transcriptions of all these sketch pages will be found in Susan Filler's dissertation.[6] Example 19 begins at what would be two bars before cue 19 in the final version of the first movement.

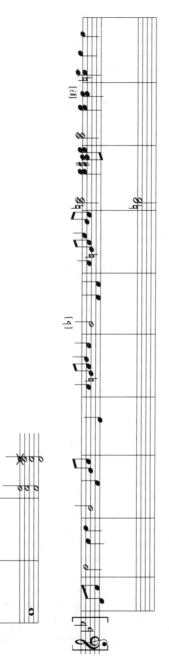

Example 18

103

[reduced from four staves]

C-DUR

[etc.]

Example 19

Notes

Preface

1 *The Face*, no. 79 (November 1986), pp. 76–8.
2 Adorno, *Mahler*, p. 13.
3 See the report by William Mann in *The Musical Times*, Vol.102/1418 (April 1961), pp. 234–5. He observes that readers will be able to discover this 'great symphony' for themselves 'when Bruno Walter's recording is issued later this year'. The first performance of the Third at a Henry Wood Promenade Concert took place in 1963.

1 Background

1 Kokoschka, *My Life*, p. 183.
2 Sigmund Freud, 'Scientific Interest in Psychoanalysis', *The Standard Edition of the Complete Psychological Works of Sigmund Freud*, Vol.XIII (London 1955), p. 187.
3 Kokoschka, *My Life*, p. 25.
4 For example: Allan Janik and Stephen Toulmin, *Wittgenstein's Vienna* (London 1973); Carl E. Schorske, *Fin de Siècle Vienna* (New York 1980); Peter Vergo, *Art in Vienna 1898–1918* (London 1975); Robert Pynsent (ed.), *Decadence and Innovation, Austro-Hungarian Life and Art at the Turn of the Century* (London 1989).
5 Particularly relevant here is Schumann's 1835 piece, 'Florestan's Shrovetide Oration'. See Henry Pleasants (trans. and ed.), *The Musical World of Robert Schumann* (London 1965), pp. 31–4.
6 See Richard Leppert and Susan McClary (eds), *Music and Society: The Politics of Composition, Performance and Reception* (Cambridge 1987), p. xii. Adorno's *Mahler* will be further referred to: the relevant books by the other mentioned writers are William Weber, *Music and the Middle Class: The Social Structure of Concert Life in London, Paris and Vienna* (London 1975) and Marc Weiner: *Arthur Schnitzler and the Crisis of Musical Culture* (Heidelberg 1986).
7 I deliberately allude to Alexander Goehr's felicitous description of the Romantic symphony as developed from the model of Haydn and Mozart. In the first of his 1987 Reith Lectures, *The Survival of the Symphony*, 1. 'The old warhorse', The Listener, Vol.118, no.3038 (19 November 1987), p. 17, he notes: 'The *dramatis personae* of the period come to life in the music. Soldier, cleric, peasant and nobleman fight, march, love and die there.'
8 Eduard Hanslick, *The Beautiful in Music*, trans. Gustav Cohen (Indianapolis 1957), p. 125. Hanslick's comment about historical context will be found on pp. 62–3.
9 Bauer-Lechner, *Recollections*, p. 64. The other comment will be found on p. 61; both come from her record of a conversation with Mahler of 4 July 1896.
10 Letter of 1902 to Josef Krug-Waldsee; H. Blaukopf (ed.), *Gustav Mahler Briefe*, p. 275. The translation in Martner (ed.), *Selected Letters*, p. 267 is misleading. I will refer throughout to

Herta Blaukopf's 1982 edition of the letters, which contain the fullest and most up-to-date texts of the originals, not least where I correct or attempt to improve upon the frequently inadequate translations in the Martner edition.

11 See below, p. 22-3.

12 Bauer-Lechner, *Recollections,* p. 40.

13 Ibid.

14 Henry A. Lea, *Gustav Mahler, Man on the Margin* (Bonn 1985), p. 14.

15 See Select bibliography.

16 See Zweig, *The World of Yesterday,* p. 37 and McGrath, *Dionysian Art,* p. 20.

17 Specifically *Die Welt als Wille und Vorstellung,* Vol, 1 (first published in 1818). Mahler's relationship to Schopenhauer's philosophy is discussed in Franklin, *The Idea of Music,* Ch.1, pp. 1-17 and Floros, *Gustav Mahler,* Vol. 1, pp. 152-6.

18 McGrath, *Dionysian Art,* p. 62.

19 McGrath, *Dionysian Art,* p. 80. See also p. 65, concerning Lipiner's 1877 *Leseverein* report on 'Schopenhauer as Educator'. Further reference to, and quotation from, Lipiner's lecture 'On the Elements of a Renewal of Religious Ideas in the Present' will be found in Hefling, 'Mahler's *Todtenfeier'*, pp. 28-9.

20 de La Grange, *Mahler,* Vol.1, p. 51.

21 Ibid., p. 72.

22 McGrath, *Dionysian Art,* p. 89.

23 Ibid., p. 101.

24 Bauer-Lechner, *Recollections,* p. 23. For information concerning Natalie Bauer-Lechner's later imprisonment following the publication in 1918 of an anti-war article preaching socialism and feminism, see 1984 edition of the full original typescript of *Recollections*: Bauer-Lechner (ed. Killian), *Gustav Mahler,* pp. 12-13. See Bibliography for full details.

25 This description was attributed to Franz Schmidt by Hans Keller. See Harold Truscott, *The Music of Franz Schmidt,* Vol.1: The Orchestral Music (London 1984), p. 16.

26 See Pfohl, *Gustav Mahler,* p. 58.

27 Ibid., p. 16.

28 E.T.A. Hoffmann, *The Life and Opinions of Kater Murr,* Vol. II of *Selected Writings of E.T.A. Hoffmann,* ed. and trans. by Leonard J. Kent and Elizabeth C. Knight (Chicago and London 1969), p. 63.

29 Ibid., p. 19.

30 See Martner (ed), *Selected Letters,* p. 190 (Letter 174). This translation is based on the text as revised in H. Blaukopf (ed.), *Gustav Mahler Briefe,* p. 164-5 (and note p. 165). Mahler was writing in July 1896.

31 Martner (ed.), *Selected Letters,* p. 54, translations amended according to the text in H. Blaukopf (ed.), *Gustav Mahler Briefe,* p. 8.

32 See Martner (ed.), *Selected Letters,* p. 412, Letter 105, note (b). My version follows the original German and emphasis of Alma Mahler's note in *Gustav Mahler Briefe,* ed. Alma Maria Mahler (Berlin/Vienna/Leipzig 1925), p. 126.

33 Ibid.

34 Wagner, *Beethoven,* p. 30.

35 Ibid., p. 72.

36 Ibid., p. 107.

37 Bauer-Lechner, *Recollections,* p. 38.

38 Specht, *Gustav Mahler,* p. 38.

39 Alma Mahler, *Gustav Mahler, Memories and Letters,* p. 19.

40 See Martner (ed.), Selected Letters, p. 179, translation amended according to the text in H. Blaukopf (ed.), *Gustav Mahler Briefe,* p. 149.

41 See Martner (ed.), *Selected Letters,* pp. 148-9. The translation follows that in Mitchell, *Gustav Mahler, The Wunderhorn Years,* pp. 390-1.

42 Nietzsche, *The Case of Wagner*, pp. 166, 167 and 178.

43 See Martner (ed.), *Selected Letters*, p. 140 (the letter was wrongly dated '1894' in the first German edition). See also Bauer-Lechner, *Recollections*, p. 73, where it is indicated that Mahler was still reading Nietzsche in late 1896.

44 Nietzsche, *The Birth of Tragedy*, p. 67.

45 Nietzsche, *The Gay Science*, p. 116.

46 Walter, *Gustav Mahler*, p. 129.

47 Nietzsche, *Thus spoke Zarathustra*, pp. 237-8.

48 Specht, *Gustav Mahler*, p. 73. He quotes Mahler as proclaiming: 'We all return. Life only has meaning through this certainty ... *For this reason* I have to live ethically in order to spare my returning soul some part of its journey'.

49 Nietzsche, *The Birth of Tragedy*, p. 52.

50 Ibid., p. 53. Arnim and Brentano's collection, dedicated to Goethe, was a representative document of Romantic interest in 'folk' art. Although many of their poems and song-texts were recorded from oral sources, it is assumed that their own creative preoccupations played a part in the preparation of the texts as printed. The collection's title was taken from the first poem it contains.

51 Alma Mahler, *Gustav Mahler, Memories and Letters*, p. 213.

52 See Martner (ed.), *Selected Letters*, p. 212 (the February 1897 letter to Arthur Seidl referred to in the following chapter) and H. Blaukopf (ed.), *Gustav Mahler Briefe*, p. 200.

53 See Martner (ed.), *Selected Letters*, pp. 179-80 (from the 'parting of the ways' letter to Marschalk of March 1896, quoted on p. 15 above); also Pfohl, *Gustav Mahler*, p. 54.

2 Reception

1 de La Grange, *Mahler*, Vol.1, p. 651.

2 I should like to echo Hans Eggebrecht's suggestion that no contemporary critic of Mahler can justifiably avoid engaging with Adorno (see Eggebrecht, *Die Musik Gustav Mahlers*, p. 8). The nature and scope of the present handbook permits only limited direct reference to this challenging study, but an English translation is forthcoming. Valuable quotations from Adorno's sections on *Das Lied von der Erde* appear in Mitchell, *Gustav Mahler, Songs and Symphonies of Death*, pp. 442, 444-5, 446-7, 451-2, 466 and 492.

3 Adorno, *Mahler*, pp. 55, 50 and 36. The latter observation was, of course, vehemently anticipated in any number of anti-semitic denunciations of Mahler. Rudolf Louis, in 1909, described his music as being of a variety which '*acts* Jewish. This is to say it speaks musical German, but with an accent, with an inflection, and above all, with the gestures of an eastern, all too eastern Jew.' See Nicholas Slonimsky, *Lexicon of Musical Invective*, (Seattle/London 1878), p. 121.

4 Schiedermair, *Gustav Mahler*, p. 5. Moravian and Bohemian Jews, powerful in liberal Viennese bourgeois culture, were in fact generally distinguished in the period from the poorer, more widely denigrated 'Ostjuden' alluded to in the quotation from Rudolf Louis in n.3 above.

5 Schiedermair, *Gustav Mahler*, p. 13.

6 'Great star! What would your happiness be, if you had not those for whom you shine!' and 'But we waited for you every morning, took from your superfluity and blessed you for it.' (Translations taken from Nietzsche, *Thus spoke Zarathustra*, p. 39.)

7 Although listed in the National Union Catalogue as '1901', like Schiedermair's book, the latter indicates that Seidl's *Moderner Geist* had in fact first appeared in 1900. Subsequent quotations here will be from the 1912-13 edition.

8 Schiedermair, *Gustav Mahler*, pp. 13-14.

9 Schiedermair, *Gustav Mahler,* p. 13. See also Bauer-Lechner (ed. Killian), *Gustav Mahler,* pp. 170-1.

10 Seidl, *Moderner Geist,* p. 60. The letter appears as no. 205 in Martner (ed.), *Selected Letters,* pp. 212-14.

11 Bauer-Lechner, (ed. Killian), *Gustav Mahler,* p. 171.

12 See Seidl, *Moderner Geist,* pp. 34ff.

13 Ibid., p. 38.

14 Ibid., p. 40.

15 Nietzsche, *The Case of Wagner,* p. 159.

16 I am indebted to Donald Mitchell, who kindly supplied me with a photo-copy of this pro-gramme. A photograph of Mahler's handwritten draft for the note, with the music examples, is included (facing p. 137) in Mitchell, *Gustav Mahler, The Wunderhorn Years;* it is transcribed and discussed there on pp. 318-20.

17 de La Grange, *Mahler,* Vol. 1, p. 399.

18 The translation is that of H.M. Schott in 'The Symphony since Beethoven', *Weingartner on Music and Conducting* (New York 1969), p. 283.

19 See the letters of 1900 and 1901 from Strauss to Mahler published by Edward R. Reilly in 'An Addendum to the Mahler-Strauss Correspondence', *19th Century Music,* Vol. 12/1 (Summer 1988), pp. 25-6; also those in H. Blaukopf (ed.), *Gustav Mahler, Richard Strauss,* pp. 48-59. Alma Mahler's account of the rehearsals and first performance of the Third, and Strauss's apparent 'coolness' towards Mahler (although he had been demonstrative in his approval of the symphony's first movement), will be found in Alma Mahler, *Gustav Mahler* (1973), pp. 38-42.

20 See Herta Blaukopf's essay 'Rivalry and Friendship' in H. Blaukopf (ed.), *Gustav Mahler, Richard Strauss,* pp. 117ff. Karl Franz Brendel had become the first president of the *Allgemeine Deutsche Musikverein* in 1861, having been instrumental, with Liszt, in organizing the 1859 *Tonkünstler-Versammlung* to mark the twenty-fifth anniversary of the Leipzig *Neue Zeitschrift für Musik.* The ADM developed out of that festival.

21 *The Musical Times,* Vol.43/713 (1 July 1902), p. 481. This report's list of the titles of some of the other works performed in the Festival could help explain why Mahler suppressed his own programmatic titles for the Third. A group of 'Nature'-inspired works included Schillings's *Meergruss,* Leo Blech's *Waldwanderung* and, most interestingly, Hermann Bischoff's orches-tral idyll, *Pan.*

22 See de La Grange, *Mahler,* Vol. 1, p. 399 and n.22, p. 902.

23 The (undated) letter is quoted in K. Blaukopf, *Mahler,* p. 225.

24 The plot is further thickened: (a) by an absolutism-orientated letter to Schiedermair about the Fourth Symphony from Bruno Walter, written on Mahler's behalf in response to questions about its programme (see Bruno Walter, *Briefe,* pp. 46-52); (b) by the public rebuke of Schiedermair for 'mistakes' and incipient programmaticism in his notes by Ernst Otto Nodnagel (ibid., p. 262; Nodnagel (1870-1909) was a critic and writer on music who sup-ported Mahler and wrote about him from 1902); and (c) by Mahler's angrily dismissive reac-tion to Nodnagel's own subsequently published, elaborately non-programmatic analysis (ibid.; see the short account of Nodnagel's analysis in Namenwirth, *Gustav Mahler,* Vol. 1, p. 56 (item 74)).

25 The reader is strongly recommended to study the full range of reviews cited by de La Grange. He only occasionally gives original German; translations are therefore from his own French translations in *Gustav Mahler, Chronique,* Vols. II and III. Since it has not proved fea-sible to retrace his steps and obtain the originals of all these reviews, I have tended where pos-sible to concentrate on matters of general tone and attitude.

26 *Krefelder Zeitung.* The above comments derive from articles in the *Niederrheinische Volkszeitung,* the *Krefelder Zeitung* and the Munich *Neueste Nachrichten* (Rudolf Louis). See de La Grange, *Gustav Mahler, Chronique,* Vol. II, pp. 266-9.

27 *Die Musik.* The above comments derive from the *Niederrheinische Volkszeitung*, the Munich *Neueste Nachrichten* (Rudolf Louis), and the *Allgemeine Musick-Zeitung*. See de La Grange, *Gustav Mahler, Chronique,* Vol. II, ibid.

28 See de La Grange, *Gustav Mahler Chronique,* Vol. II, p. 387. The source is Reeser, *Gustav Mahler und Holland,* p. 12. Mengelberg, director of the Concertgebouw Orchestra in Amsterdam, had attended the first performance of the Third in Crefeld and apparently invited Mahler, then or soon after, to conduct the work in Amsterdam (22 and 23 October 1903). It was given there without any indication of programmatic intention or content (the programme-book did, however, publish the text of the 'Wunderhorn' source song for the third movement). The same applied for the first performance of the symphony in Holland in Arnheim, on 17 October 1903 under Heuckeroth.

29 Reeser, *Gustav Mahler und Holland,* p. 9. Letter from Diepenbrock to J. C. Hol of 30 October 1903.

30 Ibid., pp. 9-10.

31 de La Grange, *Gustav Mahler, Chronique,* Vol. II, pp. 392-3.

32 Ibid., p. 410.

33 Ibid., pp. 412-13.

34 Ibid., p. 413.

35 Ibid., p. 526.

36 See Mahler's 1902 letter to Richard Braungart, quoted in de La Grange, *Gustav Mahler, Chronique,* Vol. II, p. 260.

37 Ibid., p. 404.

38 Ibid., p. 416.

39 Ibid., pp. 529-30.

40 Ibid., pp. 531 and 533-4.

41 Ibid., pp. 536-7.

42 Ibid., p. 539. A letter from Schoenberg to Mahler of December 1904, apparently recording impressions of the Third, appears in Alma Mahler, *Gustav Mahler* (1973), pp. 256-7.

43 See de La Grange, *Gustav Mahler, Chronique,* Vol. II, p. 990. In Bekker, *Gustav Mahlers Sinfonien* (p. 358), we learn that the programme was printed in the concert-brochure, with an explanatory note by Mahler, for the Berlin Philharmonic performance of the Third in 1907 (1 January, Mahler conducting).

44 de La Grange, *Gustav Mahler, Chronique,* Vol. III, pp. 542-5. The original appeared as part of the 'Feuilleton' ('Zwei Mahler-Sinfonien') on pp. 1-3 of the *Wiener Abendpost,* 5 November 1909 (no. 254). The second part of the article was devoted to the Seventh Symphony. The translation here is based on the original source.

3 Genesis and design

1 Bauer-Lechner, *Recollections,* p. 40.

2 Susan Filler, 'Editorial Problems in Symphonies of Gustav Mahler' (1976). Unfortunately, neither the present author nor John Williamson were aware of this dissertation while carrying out related work at much the same time; see Franklin, 'The Gestation of Mahler's Third Symphony' (1977) and Williamson, 'Mahler's Compositional Process' (1980). Filler's account of the known sketch material was brought up to date in Reilly, 'A Re-examination of the Manuscripts of Mahler's Third Symphony'. Newly recovered are an early sketch for mov. 5, a titled sketch and a orchestral draft for mov. 2, a sketch for mov. 3. F Krummacher (1990, see Bibliography) has added fresh insights.

3 See also the interesting discussion of earlier, five-movement programme-symphonies in Floros, *Gustav Mahler,* Vol. II, pp. 48-51.

4 The most concise interpretation of the Third as a utopian expression of radical politics will

be found in Schnebel, 'Sinfonie und Wirklichkeit'.

5 See Adorno, *Mahler*, pp. 104-5.

6 Bauer-Lechner, *Recollections*, p. 32.

7 Alma Mahler, *Gustav Mahler, Memories and Letters*, p. 213; translation amended in accordance with Alma Mahler, *Gustav Mahler, Erinnerungen*, p. 268.

8 See Martner (ed.), Selected Letters, p. 180; translation amended in accordance with H. Blaukopf (ed.), *Gustav Mahler Briefe*, p. 150.

9 Schopenhauer, *The World as Will and Representation*, Vol. II, p. 581.

10 Ibid., p. 60. The dissolute Ixion, in Greek mythology, was punished for attempting to seduce Hera, wife of Zeus. He was bound to a wheel of fire that rolled ceaselessly across the sky.

11 Bauer-Lechner, *Recollections*, p. 67.

12 Nietzsche, *The Gay Science*, p. 32.

13 de La Grange, *Mahler*, Vol. I, p. 686.

14 de La Grange, *Mahler*, Vol. I, p. 362. Mahler had formerly used this phrase, probably alluding to Goethe, in 1888 (see H. Blaukopf (ed.), *Gustav Mahler Briefe*, p. 66 (Letter 65) and Hefling, 'Mahler's *Todtenfeier*', p. 30).

15 Bauer-Lechner, *Recollections*, p. 30 (and see p. 231).

16 See Bekker, *Gustav Mahlers Sinfonien*, p. 106 and Alma Mahler, *Gustav Mahler, Memories and Letters*, pp. 38-9 (Alma Mahler, *Gustav Mahler, Erinnerungen*, p. 53). The differences are discussed in Susan Filler, 'Editorial Problems in Symphonies of Gustav Mahler', pp. 37-8.

17 See *Lieder eines fahrenden Gesellen*, song no. 2:' "... isn't it a beautiful world? / Hey you! Well? Beautiful world!" / Will my happiness really begin now? / No! No! I think / it can never, never flower in me.' See also Bauer-Lechner, *Recollections*, p. 63, where Mahler speaks of having wanted to 'relax' with the Third after the 'seriousness and weightiness of the Second'.

18 de La Grange, *Mahler*, Vol. I, p. 250.

19 Again based on the version in Bekker, *Gustav Mahlers Sinfonien*, p. 106.

20 See my transcription in Appendix II, which agrees in all but a few minor details with that in Susan Filler, 'Editorial Problems in Symphonies of Gustav Mahler', p. 598. See also Bauer-Lechner, *Recollections*, plate facing p. 64 and p. 67 (also p. 203, n. 30).

21 See de La Grange, *Mahler*, Vol. I, pp. 269 (where it is interestingly noted that Viktor Adler and Engelbert Pernerstorfer spent *their* summers, too, on the opposite shore of the Attersee) and 278.

22 The relevant page is the first of the second set of sketches in Stanford University Library, the page bearing the date (hand unknown) '1895'. See also Franklin, 'The Gestation of Mahler's Third Symphony', pp. 441 and 443. The heading was in fact referred to in the original German edition of Natalie Bauer-Lechner, *Erinnerungen an Gustav Mahler* (Leipzig/Vienna/Zurich 1923), note on p. 20, where it is made evident that these sketches were indeed part of her 'Nachlass'. The page is reproduced in Floros, *Gustav Mahler*, Vol. III, p. 330.

23 Mitchell, *Gustav Mahler, The Wunderhorn Years*, pp. 252-3 (n.21) and p. 257 (n.27). The draft, present location unknown, is described in Reilly, 'A Re-examination of the Manuscripts of Mahler's Third Symphony', pp. 62-4.

24 The draft is now in the Pierpont Morgan Library, New York (Mary Flagler Cary Collection).

25 Martner (ed.), *Selected Letters*, p. 163 (no. 136) (see H. Blaukopf (ed.), *Gustav Mahler Briefe*, p. 126 (no. 145) and Martner (ed.), *Selected Letters*, pp. 164-5 (no. 137) (see H. Blaukopf (ed.), *Gustav Mahler Briefe*, pp. 127-8 (no. 146)).

26 Letter to Marschalk of 6 August 1896 (Martner (ed.), *Selected Letters*, p. 192, no. 178); but note that Mahler reverted to 'Morgentraum' in the programme-note for the concert on 9 November 1896 (see above, p. 24).

27 Both poems are reproduced in Floros, *Gustav Mahler*, Vol. I, pp. 203-8. See also ibid., pp. 82-83 and Vol. III, p. 82. The most extended treatment of Nietzsche's influence on Mahler will be found in Nikkels, *'O Mensch! Gib Acht!'*.

28 See below pp. 77 and 84–5.

29 See Martner (ed.), *Selected Letters*, pp. 164–5 (no. 137). The translation follows more closely that in Mitchell, *Gustav Mahler, The Wunderhorn Years*, p. 169. Mahler abbreviates the titles of the movements (e.g. 'W. die Tiere m. e.') as indicated in Martner, but the best text is that in H. Blaukopf (ed.), *Gustav Mahler Briefe*, pp. 127–8 (no. 146), which restores Mahler's excited emphasis as reproduced here.

30 See H. Blaukopf (ed.), *Gustav Mahler Briefe*, pp. 165–8 (and note), where a fuller version of the previously edited-down letter to Anna von Mildenburg is given. Compare the original version of Alma Mahler (ed.), *Gustav Mahler Briefe* 1879-1911 (Berlin/Vienna Leipzig 1924 and 1925) no. 153, pp. 162–3, with Martner (ed.), *Selected Letters*, p. 190 (no. 174). In the fuller Blaukopf text, Mahler again lists the movement-titles, beginning: 'I. Was mir das Felsgebirge erzählt; / II. *Der Sommer marschiert ein!*'

31 It is in this letter of 1 July 1896 that Mahler tells 'dear Annerl' that Love (alluding to the movement's actual subtitle) is telling him very beautiful things: 'when it speaks to me at the moment it always tells me of you! – But in the symphony, dear Anni, it is a question of another kind of love than the one you are imagining.' The letter is partly restored in Martner (ed.), *Selected Letters*, p. 188 (no. 169), but again the fullest version is in H. Blaukopf (ed.), *Gustav Mahler Briefe*, p. 166 (no. 181).

32 Nietzsche, *The Gay Science*, p. 200 (III, Section 166).

33 The explicit direction 'Grob' ('coarse' or 'crude') appears at cue 23 in the third movement.

34 Nietzsche, *Thus spoke Zarathustra*, p. 55.

35 Ibid., p. 157.

36 Ibid., p. 40.

37 Bauer-Lechner, *Recollections*, p. 60.

38 Ibid., p. 62.

39 Ibid., p. 64.

40 See Franklin, 'The Gestation of Mahler's Third Symphony', p. 445 and Mitchell, *Gustav Mahler, The Wunderhorn Years*, pp. 313ff, where the Minuet reference is tentatively considered on p. 315. Mahler's comment to Natalie about the generative role of *Das himmlische Leben* with respect to Symphony III was recorded in a formerly unpublished part of her memoir. De La Grange (the owner of her original manuscript) transcribed the relevant passage (de La Grange, Mahler, Vol. I, p. 249) as suggesting that the song had given birth to 'five pieces of the *Third* and *Fourth Symphonies*'. H. Killian's version (from the publisher's typescript) is less explicit. There Mahler refers to the rich crop of music stemming from the song as including 'whole symphonic movements [ganze Symphonie-Sätze] in the Third and Fourth'; see Bauer-Lechner (ed. Killian), *Gustav Mahler*, p. 172.

41 See Bauer-Lechner, *Recollections*, p. 154 (1900).

42 See H. Blaukopf (ed.), *Mahler's Unknown Letters*, p. 123 (German edition: *Gustav Mahler. Unbekannte Briefe* (Vienna/Hamburg 1983), p. 127).

43 It was in *Die fröhliche Wissenschaft* that Nietzsche announced 'God is dead' (see Nietzsche, *The Gay Science*, Section 108, p. 167), going on in Section 125 (ibid., p. 181) to add '*We have killed him* – you and I.'

44 Nietzsche, *The Gay Science*, Section 337, pp. 268–9.

4 The music

1 Bekker, *Gustav Mahlers Sinfonien*, p. 120.

2 Bauer-Lechner, *Recollections*, p. 64.

3 Bekker, *Gustav Mahlers Sinfonien*, p. 120.

4 Ibid., p. 122.
5 See his letter of 26 March 1896 to Marschalk, where he describes the second and third movements of the Second 'als Interludium gedacht' (H. Blaukopf (ed.), *Gustav Mahler Briefe*, p.
   150).
6 Bauer-Lechner, *Recollections*, p. 52 (and 233).
7 See Martner (ed.), *Selected Letters*, p. 197 (and H. Blaukopf (ed.), *Gustav Mahler Briefe*, pp.
   179-80).
8 Donald Mitchell discusses the evidence of a 'generative' influence upon the Third of *Das
   himmlische Leben* in Mitchell, *Gustav Mahler, The Wunderhorn Years*, pp. 312ff. He notes the
   second movement reference on p. 315. Bar-numbers in the song should be taken to refer to
   the final movement of the Fourth Symphony. The *Wunderhorn* poem describes 'The
   Heavenly Life' as one of childlike merriment and gastronomic indulgence. But in the shadows Herod kills the lamb and St Luke butchers oxen. St Peter nevertheless obligingly catches fish from the celestial pond while heavenly music convinces us that 'all things awaken to
   joy'.
9 Bauer-Lechner, *Recollections*, p. 52. Mengelberg's conducting-score seems to reflect similar
   conversations with Mahler. At the end (p. 132, bar 267) Mengelberg writes over the glockenspiel notes: 'Sterbeglöcklein / die Blumen sterben' ('little death-knell / the flowers die').
10 As Mahler described it in a letter of November 1896 to Annie Sommerfeld; see de La
   Grange, *Mahler*, Vol. I, p. 386. The 1896 manuscript of the movement concludes with an
   inscription following the date: 'Hamburg 11 April 96 (In doloribus / In dolores)'. The gloomy
   mood was in all likelihood a product of tension and unhappiness in his relationship with Anna
   von Mildenburg (ibid., pp. 359-60).
11 Bauer-Lechner, *Recollections*, p. 129 (translation amended).
12 By Edith Braun. See *Mahler: 24 Songs for Voice and Piano* (New York n.d.), Vol. III, p. ii. It
   is interesting to note that the first orchestral draft of this movement (Pierpont Morgan
   Library, Mary Flagler Cary Collection) has the first flute (not piccolo) shadow more closely
   the vocal line of the song's opening, with its repeated notes, than is the case in the final version.
13 'Wie aus weiter Ferne'. All such directions subsequently quoted are translations of annotations
   in the published score, unless otherwise indicated. Concerning the posthorn itself, the first
   orchestral draft of this movement could be taken as evidence that the 'programmatic' conception of the movement did indeed come as a 'final ideal clarification'. Although the
   posthorn melody is present as in the final version, it is played by the trumpet in F (which
   continues from eight before cue 14) with no mention of any other instrument or 'distance'
   direction. Mahler subsequently decided to have a Flügelhorn play the relevant parts (indicated in the final manuscript and first Weinberger edition of the score; see also Bauer-Lechner,
   Recollections, p. 61). Finally, an actual 'posthorn in B flat' was specified. It might also be noted
   that the first draft mentioned here has two trumpets at bar 466, while the solo at cue 29 is
   directed to be 'hinter der Szene'.
14 Unless otherwise stated, 'the manuscript' will refer to the 1896 fair-copy in The Pierpont
   Morgan Library, New York, property of Robert O. Lehmann (see Appendix I).
15 See Eggebrecht, *Die Musik Gustav Mahlers*, Ch. 5, 'Die Posthorn Episode', pp. 169-97.
16 Adorno, *Mahler*, p. 55. The two main sections in which Adorno discusses the movement are
   pp. 16-18 and pp. 54-5. On the matter of the derivative nature of the melody, Eggebrecht is
   illuminating. He suggests a number of 'sources', including the *dolce grazioso* melody from
   Liszt's *Rhapsodie Espagnole* which the posthorn seems directly to quote for four bars from
   nine after cue 15 (*Die Musik Gustav Mahlers*, p. 183).
17 'Zusammenhang der Aussage': Eggebrecht, *Die Musik Gustav Mahlers*, p. 197.
18 Ibid., p. 191.
19 See Lebrecht, *Mahler Remembered*, p. 257 and de La Grange, *Gustav Mahler, Chronique*, Vol.
   II, p. 991, n. 189.

20 Floros (*Gustav Mahler* Vol. III, pp. 94-5) suggests that another Lenau piece, 'Die Posthorn', is also relevant here.

21 See Eggebrecht, *Die Musik Gustav Mahlers*, p. 195. Mahler's early memories of Prague's Vlassim Park have also been linked with this movement (see de La Grange, *Mahler*, Vol. I, p. 897, n. 64).

22 My translation is based on the German text in Carl Hepp (ed.), *Lenaus Werke* (Leipzig/Vienna n.d.), pp. 102-3. 'Das Posthorn', mentioned by Floros (see n. 20 above), will be found on pp. 13-14.

23 'Wie die Weise eines Posthorns', the score reads. 'Weise' means 'manner' or 'style' as well as 'tune' or 'air' in the musical sense, but note Mahler's use of the term 'Volksweise' in the First Symphony: the melody after cue 10 in the third movement is marked 'Sehr einfach und schlicht wie eine Volksweise'.

24 de La Grange, *Mahler*, Vol. I, p. 399, quoting Paul Moos's review which cites the programme in the following manner: 'the animals are roving the forest, happy and carefree, when man appears and walks calmly by. At once a sudden terror grips the animals, because "they guess the peril that man represents for their lives".'

25 Eggebrecht, *Die Musik Gustav Mahlers*, p. 196.

26 Schopenhauer, *The World as Will and Representation*, Vol. II, p. 61.

27 The precise formula occurs in the plan as follows:

SINFONIE NR 4 (HUMORESKE)

Nr.1.   Die Welt als ewige Jetztzeit, G-dur [The world as eternal present, G major].

Nr.2.   Das irdische Leben, es-moll [E flat minor].

Nr.3.   Caritas H-Dur [B major] (Adagio).

Nr.4.   Morgenglocken, F-Dur [F major].

Nr.5.   Die Welt ohne Schwere, D-dur (Scherzo). [The world without gravity, D major].

Nr.5.   [sic] Das himmlische Leben, G-dur [G major].

See Bekker, *Gustav Mahlers Sinfonien*, p. 358. He describes the plan as having been written on a 'large-quarto-format' sheet which 'apparently belonged originally with the comparable early sketch-page for the Third' (the first of the two early plans — see above p. 42 — is meant).

28 Bauer-Lechner, *Recollections*, p. 59 and see p. 234 (translations slightly amended).

29 The first (1895?) orchestral draft (Pierpont Morgan Library, Mary Flagler Cary Collection) shows that Mahler's initial version of this outburst was simpler. Above arpeggiated string accompaniment (E flat minor), the trombones play their motif as in bars 545-8 in the printed score, but then repeat it, the last B flat being sustained, with no movement to D flat.

30 Adorno, *Mahler*, p. 17. Note also Adorno's reference to the movement's portent of 'catastrophes which could quickly bring the forest in to swallow up the devastated cities' — a reading of the movement's darker side which highlights the relative innocence of Specht's description of it as a 'charming piece, like a Schwind painting in music' (Specht, *Mahler III Symphonie*, p. 20). Both, in their way, say something valuable about this movement.

31 Bauer-Lechner, *Recollections*, p. 129.

32 Nietzsche, *Thus spoke Zarathustra*, p. 328 (see also pp. 243-4); cf. Nietzsche, *Also sprach Zarathustra* (Stuttgart 1983), p. 306.

33 The first orchestral draft show various experiments with metre and the use of rests, with or without pause-marks over them. The movement opens there in $\frac{4}{4}$, the initial bars then being numbered above the score to indicate the varying time-signatures required (the first seven bars read '4 6 4 4 8 4 4').

34 The translation here is my own, which aims at literal clarity rather than poetic quality: it reproduces Mahler's rearrangement of the Nietzsche original and his omission of the quotation marks. The German text is Nietzsche's, with Mahler's added line in square brackets.

35 See Floros, *Gustav Mahler*, Vol. II, p. 205.

36 See Eggebrecht, *Die Musik Gustav Mahlers*, p. 140 (in the context of an interesting essay on this movement's syntactic and semantic structure, pp. 136-44).

37 See Nietzsche, *Thus Spoke Zarathustra*, pp. 241-2.

38 I am indebted to Adorno for this thought; he quotes the poem in *Philosophie der neuen Musik* (see Adorno, *Philosophy of Modern Music*, trans. Anne G. Mitchell and Wesley V. Bloomster (London 1973), pp. 37-8, n.6). The translation is by Michael Hamburger, from Hamburger, *Friedrich Hölderlin*, pp. 44-5. As to where Hölderlin himself got the idea, it is worth noting that at the end of Virgil's *Aeneid*, Aeneas' final victory over Turnus is precipitated by Jupiter, who sends down to the battlefield one of his attendant demons. The demon shrinks 'to the form of that small bird which in the night-time perches on tombstones or deserted roof-tops and eerily sings her late song among the shadows' (trans. W. F. Jackson Knight (London 1977 etc.), pp. 335-6).

39 See Bauer-Lechner, *Recollections*, p. 64. Some of the thematic links with the first movement were clarified only after the latter's composition. The first orchestral draft and first published score have the solo violin at cue 8 approach the descending figure with an arabesque that was only later replaced by the simpler ascending scale that establishes the link with the first movement, four before cue 7 (first trumpet in F).

40 Bauer-Lechner, *Recollections*, pp. 129-30.

41 Translation by Deryck Cooke (Cooke, *Gustav Mahler*, pp. 65-6). The original, in five five-line stanzas (four plus the last words of the fourth line repeated as a fifth) will be found in Arnim and Brentano, *Des Knaben Wunderhorn*, p. 674, as 'Poor Children's Begging-Song' ('Armer Kinder Bettlerlied'). Mahler used the text more or less as he found it there, although in 1.15 he changes 'Only pray to God all the time' to 'Only love God all the time!'

42 It is to be regretted that the *Gesamtausgabe* edition of the score did not reinstate Mahler's clearly intended *paired* directions over the soprano line in bars 27-30. Where now we read sanft ('gentle', or even 'meek') at bar 30, the manuscript, sketch and first Weinberger score had all clearly added the alternative *grob* at the last beat of bar 27.

43 Like so many of Mahler's *Wunderhorn* song-texts, this epigraph is far from being a direct quotation from Arnim and Brentano. Its source is apparently an eight-line piece entitled 'Erlösung' ('Redemption') from which Mahler improvises his couplet. The full German text, with a translation, will be found in Martner (ed.), *Selected Letters*, note to Letter 137, p. 419. See Arnim and Brentano, *Des Knaben Wunderhorn*, p. 753. Webern set it, in its original form, as the second of his *Three Songs for Soprano, E flat Clarinet and Guitar*, op. 18.

44 *Die Musik* (Berlin) found 'majesty' in the Adagio to offset the 'banalities', the 'rude and garish' sounds of the earlier parts of the symphony at its first performance (see de La Grange, *Gustav Mahler, Chronique*, Vol. II, p. 269).

45 See Bekker. *Gustav Mahlers Sinfonien*, p. 133.

46 The rediscoverer and editor of this work, Paul Banks, wrote an invaluable article about it in *The Musical Times* in March 1989 (see Banks, 'Hans Rott and the New Symphony'). It included facsimiles of four of the manuscript pages from which Ex. 10 has been adapted. See Bauer-Lechner, *Recollections*, p. 146 for the most extended record of comment by Mahler on Rott, whose symphony he had taken to Maiernigg to 'look through with a view to eventual performance' in the summer of 1900.

47 Section added in Bauer-Lechner (ed. Killian), *Gustav Mahler*, p. 66.

48 See above, p. 49.

49 Bauer-Lechner, *Recollections*, p. 59 (and see p. 234). Compare the passage in Bauer-Lechner (ed. Killian), *Gustav Mahler*, p. 56.

50 Bauer-Lechner, *Recollections*, p. 38; Mahler's reference there is to the fourth stanza of 'Der Rhein'.

51 References are to the translation in Hamburger, *Friedrich Hölderlin*, pp. 409ff.

52 See Bauer-Lechner, *Recollections*, p. 64.

53 My translation follows Mahler's words as quoted in Foerster, *Der Pilger*, p. 456 (compare the typically cavalier translation in de La Grange, *Mahler*, Vol. I, p. 330).

54 Compare the programme-note of November 1896; see above. p. 24.

55 I am indebted for this observation to David B. Greene, in Greene, *Mahler, Consciousness and Temporality*, p. 140 and p. 192, n.5. The reference is to Deryck Cooke's 1960 BBC booklet on Mahler, later revised as Cooke, *Gustav Mahler*.

56. See Bauer-Lechner, *Recollections*, p. 61.

57 Ibid., p. 62.

58 See Martner (ed.), *Selected Letters*, p. 189 and H. Blaukopf (ed.), *Gustav Mahler Briefe*, p. 168. The translation here (by James Galston) is taken from Walter, *Gustav Mahler*, p. 23. I have retained the internal quotation-marks, which do not occur in the Blaukopf text.

59 See Bauer-Lechner, *Recollections*, p. 76.

60 Ibid., p. 62.

61 Ibid.

62 See Alma Mahler, *Gustav Mahler, Memories and Letters*, p. 39.

63 Bauer-Lechner, *Recollections*, p. 41.

64 See K. Blaukopf, *Mahler. A Documentary Study*, plate 135. It is, incidentally, clear from this that de La Grange (*Mahler*, Vol. I, pp. 798-9) is wrong in placing the subtitle 'Die Engel' after 'Was mir die Liebe erzählt' in his plan no. 6, dated 11 September 1895. The source would seem to be this letter, dated 'II (Roman numeral) Sept. 95' at the end. The bracketed 'Die Engel' clearly follows the title 'Was mir die Morgenglocken erzählen'.

65 Bauer-Lechner, *Recollections*, p. 59.

66 This term was used by Mahler in his description of the symphony (see, e.g., Bauer-Lechner, *Recollections*, p. 40; the word translated there variously as 'merriment' and 'gaiety' is 'Heiterkeit' in the original). J. P. Stern discusses the meaning of the word in Stern, *Nietzsche*, p. 56.

67 See Robert Graves, *The Greek Myths*: 1, revised edn (London 1960 etc.), p. 102.

68 Martner (ed.), Selected Letters, p. 190; translation amended in accordance with H. Blaukopf (ed.), *Gustav Mahler Briefe*, p. 170.

69 See Bauer-Lechner, *Recollections*, p. 63.

70 The painting is usefully described in Peter Vergo, *Art in Vienna 1898-1918*, 2nd edn (London 1981), pp. 44-5. These comments inevitably raise the question of Mahler's relationship to contemporary artistic manners like those of Jugendstil (on this see Wolfgang Schlüter, 'Die Wunde Mahler', in Metzger and Riehn (eds.), *Musik-Konzepte*, pp. 106ff). My own inclination is to associate him with the *precursors* of *Jugendstil*, and then only with caution.

71 See above, p. 29.

72 Specht, *Gustav Mahler*, p. 249.

73 See Bauer-Lechner, *Recollections*, p. 40 (translation amended). Mahler was talking here in the summer of 1895.

74 As in the case of the other movements, the internal inscriptions (see Appendix I) in the 1896 manuscript of the first movement have been listed by most commentators, e.g. Mitchell, *Gustav Mahler, The Wunderhorn Years*, p. 194. A number of the relevant pages of the manuscript are reproduced in Floros, *Gustav Mahler*, Vol. I, pp. 235-40. See also ibid., Vol. III, pp. 328-31.

75 In Walter, *Gustav Mahler*, p. 193.

76 McGrath, 'Mahler and Freud', pp. 40-51.

77 See de La Grange, *Mahler*, Vol. I, p. 803.

78 See McGrath, 'Mahler and Freud', p. 45.

79 Ibid., p. 44.

80 My source is Ludwig Erk (ed.), *Volkslieder Album. 80 Volkslieder für eine Singstimme mit Pianoforte Begleitung* (Leipzig n.d.). The song is numbered '199', suggesting that this collection was one of the many extracted from Erk's full compilation.

81 See Plate 1 and Appendix II.
82 I rely here on an undocumented additional collection of songs in the Erk edition, bound with that cited in n. 80 above in the volume belonging to The Brotherton Library, University of Leeds, p. 158.
83 The elaborate, hierarchical orchestration list in the first Weinberger score looked rather like the scene-directions for the metaphysical final scene of Goethe's Faust:

1. Holzbläser.

(a) Orchester: 1.2.3.4. Flöte – 3. u. 4. Flöte wechseln mit
1. u. 2. Piccolo. (An einer Stelle werden 4 Piccoli verwendet.)
1.2.3.4. Oboe – 4. Oboe wechselt mit Englisch Horn.
1.2.3. Clarinette in B. – 3. Clarinette wechselt mit Bassclarinette in B.
1.2. Clarinette in Es – 2. Clarinette in Es wechselt mit Clarinette in B. (1. womöglich doppelt besetzt.)
1.2.3.4. Faggott. – 4. Faggott wechselt mit Contrafagott.

2. Blechinstrumente.

1.2.3.4.5.6.7.8. Horn in F.
1.2.3.4. Trompete in F oder B (2 andere hohe Trompete womöglich zur Verstärkung heranzuziehen).
1.2.3.4. Posaune und Basstuba.

3. Schlaginstrumente.

1.2. Pauke. Je drei Pauken.
1.2. Glockenspiel (klingen eine Octave höher, als notiert).
Tambourin. – Tamtam. – Becken (freihägend, durch ein zweiter zu verstärken).
Kleine Trommel. – Grosse Trommel.
Becken (an der grossen Trommel befestigt und mit derselben von einem Musiker geschlagen).

4. Saiteninstrumente.

1.2. Harfe. – Alle Streichinstrumente sehr stark besetzt: Contrabässe mit contra C-Saite versehen)

(b) Singstimmen: Alt-Solo. – Frauenchor.
(c) In der Ferne aufgestellt: Flügelhorn in B. – Mehrere kleine Trommeln.
(d) In der Höhe postiert: Vier (eventuell 5 oder 6) abgestimmte Glocken. – Knabenchor.

Die Symphonie zerfällt in zwei Abtheilungen. Abtheil I umfasst den 1ten, Abtheilung II den 2ten, 3ten, 4ten, 5ten und 6ten Satz. Nach Abtheilung I eine grössere Pause.
84 Cooke, *Gustav Mahler*, p. 13.
85 See Greene, *Mahler, Consciousness and Temporality*, pp. 139–97.
86 Natalie Bauer-Lechner records that, on 30 July 1896, Mahler revised the opening of the first movement, doubling the number of opening bars and 'making it go at half speed in an Adagio tempo'. Inaccurate translation of the passage had led me in 1980 to speculate that the alteration was not to the opening of the 'introduction' itself. The first sentence of the relevant paragraph should surely read: 'Mahler succeeded in revising the beginning of the first movement so that it had the required effect at the head of this monumental introduction.' See McGrath's comment on this in 'Mahler and Freud', p. 46. Did Mahler experiment with doubling the note-values of the 'Weckruf' and then abandon the experiment when he made the fair-copy in September–October 1896? Interestingly, this 'primal' version of the Binzer theme sounds in fact more like the main theme of the finale of the conservative Brahms's First

Symphony than anything particularly revolutionary. Questions about musical nature are thus begged at the very outset of this work in an appropriately ambivalent way. As to the phrase *Der Weckruf* itself, the usual military translation ('Reveille') is appropriate, but possibly obscures any intended allusion to Wagner's *Siegfried* (II/1), where Wotan, as The Wanderer, hails the grandly invoked Erda with the words: 'Der Weckrufer bin ich' (see Schott vocal score, p. 245).

87 See Mitchell, *Gustav Mahler, The Wunderhorn Years*, pp. 299-300.

88 The added page in the manuscript (headed 'Einlage') is attached in such a way that it can be lifted to reveal the original. At one bar after cue 9, the texture is much as in the final version, but the horns were originally a fifth higher (sounding D, E, F). A five-bar descending chromatic slither in the cellos leads directly to (final version) seven after cue 10. The revision entailed an overall addition of four bars.

89 This is the form in which it appears in the (?1896) Vienna sketches — which continue at what is now cue 19 with the melodic line (in C major) of the accompaniment that precedes the entry of the voice in the final E major section of *Das himmlische Leben*. See Franklin, 'The Gestation of Mahler's Third Symphony' and Williamson, 'Mahler's Compositional Process'.

90 Interestingly, this might have been the earliest of all sketched versions of the material, since it corresponds with the section headed 'Pan schläft' in the 1895 Stanford sketches ('p.7'). See Franklin, 'The Gestation of Mahler's Third Symphony', p. 444. De La Grange, *Mahler*, Vol. I, p. 796, interprets the additional, subsequently scratched out inscription on the sketch at this point as 'Naturs Erwachen'. Following personal examination of the sketch, I can report that the obliterated word was in fact almost certainly 'Naturlaute' ('sounds of Nature'). Much of the material in de La Grange's appendix on the Third Symphony must be treated with great caution.

91 See Nietzsche, *Thus spoke Zarathustra*, p. 120. The German title of this section ('Of the Rabble') is 'Vom Gesindel'.

92 See Ivar Oxaal, Michael Pollack and Gerhard Botz (eds.), *Jews, Antisemitism and Culture in Vienna* (London 1987), p. 18. There is to my knowledge no indication that Nietzsche himself intended any antisemitic reading of this passage in *Zarathustra*.

93 My allusion is to one of the early programmatic titles for the First Symphony's third movement. See Stefan, *Gustav Mahler*, p. 113. This reading of the 'Gesindel' episode might be too straightforward, however. Could the passage equally represent a musical expression of a kind of antisemitism not uncommon amongst 'assimilated' Jews at this time, or at least an attitude towards the brute 'mob' that was more truly Nietzschean than Social Democratic? Evidence in support of this suggestion is found in the original manuscript of the Bauer-Lechner memoir owned by de La Grange. While working on the first movement of the Third, on 25 July 1896, Mahler was, we learn, reading not only *Don Quixote*, but also Carlyle's *Frederick the Great* and finding the latter's warlike spirit reflected in his music: 'The victorious columns of troops that instantly overthrow the enemy rabble are just like the Prussian armies. And what about the role played by both Prussian and Austrian military bands?' See de La Grange, *Mahler*, Vol. I, p. 375. This information tends to reproblematize the whole issue of the movement's expression of militaristic power, not least over Mahler's hard-pressed orchestral players, who might well have had cause to question whose side he was on. The manuscript includes, at four after cue 51, the superscription *Vorwärts stürmen!* Mahler certainly seems to have taken his identification with Frederick the Great to heart at this point!

94 See Bauer-Lechner, *Recollections*, p. 64 (translation slightly amended).

95 See Donald Mitchell's discussion of Mahler's recapitulatory process, particularly here, in Mitchell, *Gustav Mahler, The Wunderhorn Years*, pp. 206-8.

96 Bauer-Lechner, *Recollections*, p. 66.

97 From material added to the 27 July section in Bauer-Lechner (ed. Killian), *Gustav Mahler*, p. 65.

98 In 1905; see Alma Mahler, *Gustav Mahler, Memories and Letters*, p. 82.

99 See Bruno Walter, *Gustav Mahler* (Berlin 1957), p. 30. The English translation in Walter, *Gustav Mahler* (p. 24) rather clumsily renders Mahler's advice to Walter, as he arrived at Steinbach in 1896, that he need not admire the craggy face of the Höllengebirge: '... das habe ich schon alles wegkomponiert'. Compare also another comment to Natalie on 27 July 1896 cited in de La Grange, *Mahler,* Vol. I, p. 898 (from the manuscript in the author's collection).

100 'Dem der da kommen wird! / Denen die da sein werden!' See plate facing the title-page of the Philharmonia pocket score of the revised version.

Appendix II

1 See Bauer-Lechner, *Recollections,* p. 67 and Plate 3 (facing p. 64).
2 Franklin, 'The Gestation of Mahler's Third Symphony', p. 443.
3 See Bauer-Lechner, *Recollections,* p. 67 (and note 30). In my editorial annotations to the *Recollections* in 1980, I failed to refer to the note in the first edition of the Bauer-Lechner (Leipzig etc. 1923, p. 20) which cites the sketch of the 'flowers' movement, titled 'Was das Kind erzählt', as being 'aus dem Nachlass der Verfasserin' ('amongst the author's papers'). That sketch appears as the first of the '1895' pages ('5') referred to here.
4 Williamson, 'Mahler's Compositional Process'.
5 Franklin, 'The Gestation of Mahler's Third Symphony', p. 445.
6 Filler, 'Editorial Problems in Symphonies of Gustav Mahler', pp. 598-608.

Select bibliography

Adorno, Theodor, *Mahler, Eine musikalische Physiognomik* (Frankfurt 1978 [1960])

Arnim, L. Achim von and Brentano, Clemens. *Des Knaben Wunderhorn*. Alte Deutsche Lieder (Munich 1957)

Banks, Paul. 'Mahler's Todtenfeier : a Symphonic Poem?' *The Musical Times*, Vol. 129/1750 (December 1988)

'Hans Rott and the New Symphony', *The Musical Times*, Vol. 130/1753 (March 1989)

Bauer-Lechner, Natalie. *Recollections of Gustav Mahler*, trans. Dika Newlin, ed. Peter Franklin (London 1980)

Gustav Mahler in den Erinnerungen von Natalie Bauer-Lechner, ed. Herbert Killian (Hamburg 1984)

Bekker, Paul. *Gustav Mahler Sinfonien*, reprint of the 1921 edition (Tutzing 1969)

Blaukopf, Herta (ed.). *Gustav Mahler Briefe, Neuausgabe erweitert und revidiert ...* (Vienna/Hamburg 1982)

Gustav Mahler. Richard Strauss. Correspondence 1888-1911, trans. Edmund Jephcott (London 1984)

Mahler's Unknown Letters, trans. Richard Stokes (London 1986)

Blaukopf, Kurt. Mahler, A Documentary Study (London 1976)

Cooke, Deryck. *Gustav Mahler. An Introduction to his Music* (London 1980)

Eggebrecht, Hans Heinrich. *Die Musik Gustav Mahlers* (Munich 1986 [1982])

Filler, Susan M. 'Editorial Problems in Symphonies of Gustav Mahler. A Study of the Sources of the Third and Tenth Symphonies' (PhD thesis, Northwestern University 1976)

Gustav and Alma Mahler, A Guide to Research, Garland Composer Resource Manuals 28 (New York/London 1989)

Floros, Constantin. Gustav Mahler, Vol. I: *Die geistige Welt Gustav Mahlers in systematischer Darstellung* (Wiesbaden 1977); Vol. II: *Mahler und die Symphonik des 19. Jahrhunderts in neuer Deutung* (Wiesbaden 1977); Vol. III: *Die Symphonien* (Wiesbaden 1985)

Foerster, Josef Bohuslav. *Der Pilger. Erinnerungen eines Musikers* (Prague 1955)

Franklin, Peter. 'The Gestation of Mahler's Third Symphony', *Music and Letters*, Vol. 58/4 (1977)

The Idea of Music. Schoenberg and Others (London 1985)

Greene, David B. *Mahler, Consciousness and Temporality* (New York/London 1984)

Hamburger, Michael (trans.). *Friedrich Hölderlin. Poems and Fragments. Bilingual edition* (Cambridge 1980)

Select bibliography

Hefling, Stephen E. 'Mahler's *Todtenfeier* and the Problem of Program Music', *19th Century Music*, Vol. 12/1 (1988)

Kokoscha, Oskar. *My Life*, trans. David Britt (London 1974)

Krummacher, Friedhelm. 'Die wenigen Blätter und die sämtlichen Keime. Über Mahlers Skizzen zum Kopfsatz der III. Symphonie', *Neue Musik und Tradition: Festschrift Rudolf Stephan zum 65 Geburtstag*, ed. Joseph Kuckertz (Laaber 1990), pp. 347-63.

de La Grange, Henry-Louis. *Mahler*, Vol. I (London 1974)

    Gustav Mahler, Chronique d'une vie, Vol. II: *L'Age d'Or de Vienne* (Paris 1983); Vol. III: *Le Génie foudroyé* (Paris 1984)

Lebrecht, Norman. *Mahler Remembered* (London 1987)

McGrath, William J. *Dionysian Art and Populist Politics in Austria* (New Haven/London 1974)

    'Mahler and Freud: The Dream of the Stately House', in Rudolf Klein (ed.), *Gustav Mahler Kolloquium 1979 (Beiträge der Österreichischen Gesellschaft für Musik*, Vol. VII) (Kassel/Basel/London 1981), pp. 41-51

Mahler[-Werfel], Alma. *Gustav Mahler. Erinnerungen und Briefe*, 2nd edn (Amsterdam 1949 [1940])

    Gustav Mahler, Memories and Letters, trans. Basil Creighton, ed. Donald Mitchell, 3rd edn (London 1973)

Martner, Knud (ed.). *Selected Letters of Gustav Mahler*, trans. Eithne Wilkins, Ernst Kaiser and Bill Hopkins (London 1979)

Metzger, Hainz-Klaus and Riehn, Rainer (eds.). *Musik-Konzepte Sonderband. Gustav Mahler* (Munich 1989)

Mitchell, Donald. *Gustav Mahler, The Wunderhorn Years* (London 1975)

    Gustav Mahler. Songs and Symphonies of Death (London 1985)

Namenwirth, Simon Michael. *Gustav Mahler. A Critical Bibliography*, 3 vols. (Wiesbaden 1987)

Nietzsche, Friedrich. *The Birth of Tragedy* (with *The Case of Wagner*), trans. Walter Kaufmann (New York 1967)

    The Case of Wagner [see previous entry]

    The Gay Science, trans. Walter Kaufmann (New York 1974)

    Thus spoke Zarathustra. trans. R. J. Hollingdale (London 1966 [1961])

Nikkels, Eveline. *'O Mensch! Gib Acht!' Friedrich Nietzsches Bedeutung für Gustav Mahler* (Amsterdam 1989)

Pfohl, Ferdinand. *Gustav Mahler. Eindrücke und Erinnerungen aus den Hamburger Jahren*, ed. Knud Martner (Hamburg 1973)

Reeser, Eduard. *Gustav Mahler und Holland*. Briefe (Vienna 1980)

Reilly, Edward. 'A Re-examination of the Manuscripts of Mahler's Third Symphony', *Colloque Internationale Gustav Mahler 25. 26. 27. Janvier 1985* (Paris 1986), pp. 62-72

Schiedermair, Ludwig. *Gustav Mahler. Eine biographisch-kritische Würdigung* (Leipzig 1901)

Schnebel, Dieter. 'Symphonie und Wirklichkeit am Beispiel von Mahlers Dritte', in *Gustav Mahler. Sinfonie und Wirklichkeit* (Graz 1977), pp. 103-17

Schopenhauer, Arthur. *The World as Will and Representation*, trans. E. J. F. Payne, Vols. I and II (New York 1966)

Seidl, Arthur. *Moderner Geist in der deutschen Tonkunst. Gedanken eines Kulturpsychologen zur Wende des Jahrhunderts* (Regensburg n.d. (?1912-13))

Specht, Richard. *Gustav Mahler* (Berlin 1913)

    Mahler III. Symphonie D moll. Thematische Analyse (Vienna n.d.)

Stefan, Paul. *Gustav Mahler: eine Studie über Persönlichkeit und Werk* (Munich 1920)

Stern, J. P. *Nietzsche* (London 1978)

Wagner, Richard. *Beethoven*, trans. Edward Dannreuther (London 1880)

Walter, Bruno. *Briefe 1894-1962*, ed. Lotte Walter Lindt (Frankfurt am Main 1969)

    Gustav Mahler, trans. James Galston, with a biographical essay by Ernst Krenek (New York 1973)

Williamson, John. 'Mahler's Compositional Process: Reflections on an Early Sketch for the Third Symphony's First Movement'. *Music and Letters*, Vol. 61/3-4 (1980), pp. 338-45

Zweig, Stefan. *The World of Yesterday. An Autobiography*, 3rd edn (London 1944 [1943])

Index

Index

Index